# ESTONIA AND EQUINES

Finding my family and my horsey heritage

By Annabelle Till

# Acknowledgements

I should like to express my gratitude to three people.

In the first place, to the person who, whilst listening to me recounting how my mother came to this country, said, "You ought to write a book" and so unbeknownst to her, this manuscript has come into being – as it would never have been thought of or even attempted without her encouragement.

Secondly, to Stephen Masters, my Chiropractor in Barnstaple, who, for the last twenty years has put me back together on numerous occasions and kept me able to pursue my favourite sport of horse riding.

Lastly, my sincere thanks go to Lorna, whom I was lucky enough to find and who thought my tome was worth publishing, and who has constantly lifted my spirits when thanks to my piscatorial star sign, the fishes have been swimming in opposite directions, filling me with trepidation, wondering if anyone would want to read my tale of two journeys.

First published in 2014

Copyright © Annabelle Till 2014

Annabelle Till has asserted her right under the Copyright, Designs and Patents Act 1988 to be identified as the author of this work.

All rights reserved.

Editorial and Design Services by The Write Factor
www.thewritefactor.co.uk

# Contents

## PART ONE

| | |
|---|---|
| MY MOTHER | 13 |
| THE HORROR | 14 |
| HOPE | 17 |
| GROWING UP | 58 |
| WONDERING | 63 |
| SEARCHING | 65 |
| THE SEARCH FOR MY RELATIONS | 71 |
| FIRST VISIT | 78 |
| OUR SECOND VISIT TO ESTONIA IN 2009 | 99 |
| RAKVERE | 104 |
| SAD NEWS AND THIRD (UNINTENTIONAL) VISIT | 108 |
| APELSIN | 116 |
| FOURTH VISIT (INCLUDING SAAREMAA) | 120 |
| VILJANDI | 125 |
| THE EYJAFJALLAJOKULL VOLCANO | 126 |
| SAD PASSING | 130 |
| TAKING MUM HOME & ESTONIA IN THE SUMMER | 149 |
| NARVA-JÕESUU | 155 |
| 2011 – PARNU AND MUSICAL | 165 |
| MORE UNEXPECTED BAD NEWS | 167 |
| 2012 | 179 |

## PART TWO

| | |
|---|---|
| A STUBBORN INHERITANCE | 197 |
| EARLY EQUINE YEARS | 199 |
| CHOLSEBURY | 202 |
| MUSIC | 205 |
| RSPCA | 208 |
| HUNTING | 210 |
| LOSING MY BELOVED FIRST PONY | 212 |
| L'OREAL | 214 |
| SEARCHING FOR MY NEXT STEEDS | 222 |
| OYSTER (AND THE TRAILER) | 228 |
| CASHELS GRACE AND NAUGHTY BEAUTS | 232 |
| IVOR | 236 |
| GABRIEL, TAMAR, FLAUNTY & MISS GOLD | 256 |
| MOVING HOUSE (AND STABLES) | 262 |
| SPLODGE | 267 |
| TWO OLD FRIENDS RETIRE TOGETHER | 272 |
| LANCER | 277 |
| QUEEN'S CHAPLAIN – AKA CHARLIE | 285 |
| PIRATE | 291 |
| BRIGHT SPRYNGH | 294 |
| DARCO | 297 |
| JACK | 300 |
| TINTERN MEMORY | 303 |
| TINTERN TINKER | 312 |
| MY JOURNEY | 318 |

# PREFACE

The musings of a 65-year-old Cockney born, half Estonian, west-country living – 46 years and no longer a 'grockle' – woman.

The aim of this book is tell the story of my mother Astrid – who was a very strong woman – and to show what life was like in Estonia and the traumatic events that she went through to be free – something many people in this day and age will find quite incredible. I know when I first found out about this, I felt her life was something akin to a movie! I've also included some of my horsey 'reminiscing' in the book, which I hope will amuse my readers.

This book is dedicated to my wonderful Uncle Dima, my lovely cousin Marian; my husband, Ron, who loves Estonia and equines as much as I do; my father who struggled to bring Mum out of the wilderness; my grandfather, who I never knew, but gave me my love of horses; a friend who shall remain anonymous, who I have only just found in the past few years, and when needed, is always a friend indeed; and of course, Astrid, my mother, who is now re-united with her sister Maret in her homeland.

Grandfather 1927

Grandfather 1927

Grandfather in New Major's Uniform

Grandfather, Grandmother and Mum (aged 3) 1927

The whole family together with a friend in Viljandi

# PART ONE
## MY HERITAGE

# MY MOTHER

My mother Astrid was born in Estonia on 23rd April 1924 (a memorable date: St George's Day, Shakespeare's Birthday and Death Day to name but three other notable incidences). She was the oldest of three children, Maret and Allan being her younger sister and brother respectively. Incredibly this is all that I ever knew about my mother until 2007, because it upset her too much to speak about her past and relive the memories – but I have pieced together the rest in the past four years.

My mother was born in Tartu in Estonia and lived in Viljandi in her early years. I know that later she lived in Rakvere too. She grew up with a very strict father who was a Major in the Estonian Cavalry. She always loved animals, especially cats, dogs and horses, and I know that she used to love riding. Astrid, her father and her two siblings, were all living under very strict Russian occupation and later once the Russians were ousted, by Nazi Germany. All I know about my grandmother is that she ended up living in Australia with Allan. Interestingly I never liked history at school, but since learning about my Estonian background I have taken quite an interest in history and have learned so much.

# THE HORROR

Because her father was in the Estonian Army, Astrid was therefore considered a 'political' and had to be very careful about any schoolwork that she completed. Indeed, she had been pulled out of school and interrogated about pieces of work that she had written. On July 2nd 1941 Astrid's father was arrested in Rakvere and taken to a Russian concentration camp. My grandmother and my mother were beside themselves with worry, and spent a lot of time looking at mass graves trying to see if they could recognise my grandfather's corpse, as they did not know what had happened to him. I cannot begin to imagine what that must have been like and what it did to my mother and grandmother's mental health.

Unbeknownst to my mother and grandmother, my grandfather was arrested in Rakvere and taken to a Russian concentration camp in Siberia. I do not know if they found this out or not. He was sentenced to death on March 31st 1942 for starting a rebellion in the camp. When I found this out, I thought good for him! I feel I must have inherited some of his strength, and I am proud that he was a Major of the Estonian Republic and so, I gather, was he. Sadly he was executed on 8th May 1942, and the first photo I ever saw of him, which I will come to later, was his shaven head and his fingerprints from that awful camp. How life has changed everywhere and, especially now, thank God, in Estonia, although too late for my mother to go back and visit her homeland, which is something that I deeply regret.

In the early 1940s, I gather that Astrid had been made to dig trenches watched over by German guards with machine guns. Reading between the lines – from what she said over the years when she could bring herself to talk about it – I suspect that these soldiers raped her. Life became very unstable in Estonia and my mother was sent to stay with relations in Germany. Her sister, Maret, was sent to Poland to other relations, and her brother, Allan, to Finland. The family was torn apart but it was thought that this was the only way to keep them alive. In Poland, Maret married a Polish man and had a son, Igor, born in 1948. Allan, at a later date, went with his mother to live in Australia.

Something else I found out by accident and never said a word to my mother about, happened when I was newly married at around 23-years-old, when we went to Denbury in Newton Abbot, Devon, to see my parents for the weekend, as we did once a month. I needed my birth certificate and Mum told me to look through a dresser where all the certificates were kept. I came upon Mum and Dad's wedding certificate and obviously looked at it. I was shocked to see that Mum was a widow!

What on earth had happened? She was so young when she came to this country and so young to be a widow. It explained a lot to me as I had seen a couple of Mum's books, one with the name Astrid Till in it and one with the name Astrid Härm (which now I realise was her married name).

I was too young to wonder why the names were different at the time, but of course everything slotted into place in that moment that I saw the wedding certificate.

# HOPE

My father, Albert James Wallis, and his army friend, Len Nicholas, ended up in Germany in 1945, after being stationed all round the world, and while there met Astrid and her friend Ilse. I don't know how long they all went around together in Germany, but it all must have been very perilous at that time. I know that Dad and Len were staying in an old German army barracks, from which the Germans had fled and left behind their lovely horses that pulled the guns. Mum loved riding and somehow coerced Dad into going out riding with her. Dad loved animals too, but was a bit wary of the larger ones. I have a lovely picture of her and Dad wrapped in each other's arms, on two beautiful big (and I mean BIG) horses. I remember Dad saying how frightened he was because the minute they turned round to go back to the where they were stabled, his horse broke into a gallop and not being able to ride too well, it scared him to death. I think Mum loved it though.

    I didn't know it until my husband Ron found Dad's letters after both of my parents had passed away, but Dad was obviously deeply in love with Mum and moved heaven and

## Estonia and Equines

earth to get her to safety in England. Also, from these letters it appears that Mum was in a camp of some sort. I know that 'Vernons' referred to in the letters was a dog that Mum and Dad befriended and had named Vernons because she kept doing 'little pools' everywhere as a puppy (Vernons being a football pools company).

Now follows Dad's poignant letters that my husband found while renovating Mum's home after she had passed on, that are dated from March 1946 to August 1946, while he was trying to get Mum to England.

That's where Dad's letters end and the rest is what I managed to glean from my mother over the years. She had left her relations and was cleaning her attic room when Ilse rushed in and told her that Len had chartered a plane and that it was leaving in twenty minutes. So my mother, at 22 years old in 1946, left everything that she possessed and went with Ilse. She must have been so desperate to get to a country where she would be safe.

My mother, Ilse and the pilot squeezed in to a two-seater plane. I gather it had sliding back windows, and tht they had their heads stuck out of into the fresh air! Knowing in later years how scared Mum was of flying, I really can't imagine it, but I'm sure things were helped by a crate of red wine in the back of the plane! They flew to the UK under the clouds, navigating by landmarks. I really cannot begin to understand how Len managed to charter a plane or where it came from, so whether it was 'kosher' or not (as Dad would say), I don't know – and I guess Mum and Ilse didn't care. All they knew was that they were getting away to a new land and a new life.

They landed at Croydon airport, an event that I believe was reported in The Star as it was quite some feat! It seemed nobody had heard of Estonia and here there was this beautiful Estonian woman and a German woman suddenly appearing in England.

After the euphoria of landing in England and to the beginning of a new life, and thanking their lucky starts that they had made it, it must have been very frightening and daunting, as they were both whisked away to Immigration. There were communication difficulties because neither of them could speak any English, which is a bit different nowadays where everything is translated into hundreds of languages or a translator can be found at the drop of a hat.

The upshot was that both Mum and Ilse had to be married within 6 months or they would have been deported back to their respective countries, which for Mother was an unthinkable nightmare.

Len married his Ilse and had two children, John and Little Len as he was known. We saw a lot of them in my younger life. We lived in Bermondsey first of all and then Ealing and they lived in West Ham. Little Len went into the army and was killed on active service in Iraq. I found out a lot later that John was not Len's son and that Ilse had been pregnant when she came to England. Len did not know that John was not his son even on his dying day, though I personally had always wondered why they were so different. Little Len looked, sounded and acted like his father while John was tall very blond, and I know it now but I did not see it then, looked very Germanic.

Dad married his Astrid on 16th November 1946 in a registry office – Bermondsey I think – and I came along on 12th March 1948.

Mr.A.J. Harris,
463, Devon Mansions,
Tooley Street,
London, S.E.1.

Wednesday, 6 Mar 46.

My Darling,

Your hopes were certainly realised. I was home when your letter arrived, in fact it came this morning and I actually arrived in the house yesterday evening at 15 minutes to seven. The journey was very tiring and boring as you can probably imagine and I was not sorry when it was finished.

I was sorry to hear that Vernons had caused you a might loss in sleep but hope by now that she is quite at home in Frau Holthaus's house and is not causing you too much bother. I thought she might be a bit of a nuisance, which is why I stressed the fact that if she was too much work you could give her away to Willi's friend. I should imagine that round about April she'll be ahead of alot of worry, will she not? Instead of one, you'll have about nine Vernons to care for. You are very lucky!

So far I haven't had time to look for your English-German dictionary, but all in good time perhaps tomorrow I shall beable to have a good look round for you.

My Mother says that dye's are easy to get so I have asked her to buy some nigger brown, blue and black. She has already bought some coffee but has yet to find some brown thread for your rain coat. As soon as all the things are got together, I shall sendthem on to you.

Your remarks regarding the information given you by the Polish Commandant regarding Englishmen and foreigners have been noted with interest, but the more I hear of what this very intelligent man has to say themore I think he is bomb happy - now I am a long way out of his reach you can tell him I said so too (I'm only joking, Cocka!). So far, of course, I haven't had time to gather my wits about me, but as soon as everything is definite I'll let you know. Do not despair, and do not start getting thoughts of America, Africa, and all the other countries, into your head again (silly cow).

I could not quite understand the sentence written by Trudi, but please thank her for me.

And as for your letter, Darling, I must say it was a very good effort indeed and perfectly understandable throughout. If you had only carried on earlier, you would have been perfect in English by this time.

Well, my Sweet, time I was getting to bed, so I'll close now. Please give my best regards to Frau Holthaus

Yours as ever,

*all my love,*

*Bert.*

x x x x x x   (*I miss these very much indeed*)

Mr A. J. Wallis
463 Devon Mansions
Tooley St.,
London, S.E.1.

Monday 11 Mar '46

My dear Astrid,

You are probably calling me many nasty names for not keeping my promise to write to you as often as I said, but as you can no doubt imagine there is always somebody about to hinder me — they mean well enough with their good wishes, though, and as long as they mean well I'm afraid I can't say anything.

This morning I went up to the West End of London to see if I could buy any of the things in the list I wrote down for you. Sorry to say, however, that I ~~sto~~ didn't meet with much success. There were no good ~~hands~~ handbags on view — but I should be able to get one if I look enough, and I'm going out again tomorrow morning. My cousin — the one that is in that photo with me — has promised to get the buttons, thread and red belt. My mother has bought some dyes — 2 dark brown and 2 black. So as soon as I know whether it will be safe to send them through Len, I'll make up a parcel.

Although I know I should not have done so, I must confess that I had a very, very good laugh indeed when I read about Vernons. It seems that since I left she has caused you nothing but trouble. Was Mrs Stolchaus really angry or did she take the loss of her sausage in good part? I think Vernons had better look after herself or she will find herself being given away, eh?

Well, my little (?) sugar-heart, I am certainly missing you tremendously and am earnestly awaiting things to straighten out here so that I can send for you. How are the moods going, Darling — or don't you have them now? And you haven't forgotten that we are very poor, have you — nor that you must learn English very quickly,!!

Time I was getting on my way to bed. Koella.

3.

so here's sending you all my love. I'll write again on Wednesday — is that soon enough, Sweet?

All my love,
Yours as ever
Bert
xxxxxx

Please give my kind regards to Frau Stolthans.

463 Devon Mansions
Tooley St.,
London, S.E.1.

Wednesday 13 Mar 46.

My dear Astrid

Here is the letter I promised for Wednesday — You see, I do keep promises sometimes.

Yesterday I saw a Sergeant Major from my late Regiment, who has just left the army too. He told me that the Regt. is definitely moving from Vorsfelde, so you can imagine I am a little worried now regarding our communicating. If Ilsa is following Len this time perhaps you could send your letters on to her to be forwarded by Len — or can you think of a better way. Also, I have the coffee, thread, red buttons and some few cigarettes to send you — but I think I had better let these wait a while until I am certain they will reach you.

I went out again today, Darling, to look round the shops but am sorry to say that I still could not see any handbags worthy of you. Perhaps this

2.

item had better wait a little while too until you land here in England, and you can then pick one out to suit yourself.

My old firm have offered me my job back but the money they offer presents a bit of a problem. It is certainly very little. However, I am keeping my eyes open for better employment and as soon as I get good work we will try and get you to England quickly. My mother has said that if we decided to marry we could have one of her rooms — in fact my room now — until we got settled. But I would ask you not to forget, Sweetheart, that we are very poor people.

Well, my Sweet, I think it's time again for me to pinch off. Cheerio until the next time. Keep well.

All my love,
Yours as ever,
Bert.

Kindest regards to Mrs. Holtham.

I love You!! xxxxxx

463 Devon Mansions,
Tooley St.,
London, S.E.1.

Monday 19 Mar. 46.

My dear Astrid,

Thank you very much for your letter of the 9th March received this morning — my Mother brought it to me whilst I was in bed — nine o'clock, I am nearly as bad as you now!

Of course I read Churchill's speech, but you know I do not take a lot of notice of what he says!

I was pleased to learn that you had sent the large photo by post. It has not arrived yet — what did you think — is is better than the small ones?

And so nearly every day there is a Variety Show, eh? That is good!! But what about this little Englishman at the dance — don't you go and get serious with him, will you? Perhaps next time you dance with him you had better kick him in the legs instead of just treading on his feet!!

I am very glad to know that you have managed to get an English-German dictionary, etc; where did these come from — if I may ask?

Tomorrow I shall probably be sending Len on a parcel for you, containing thread, red buttons and belt, the

463 Devon Mansions
Tooley St.,
London. S.E.1.

Monday 1 April 46.

My dear Astrid,

Today I received your letter of the 27th March. Very many thanks, Gosh!

Have your feet yet recovered from the 52 kilo walk? It made my own feet tired to read your letter, goodness only knows how they would have been if they had had to do the walking!

I had a letter from Len too and he said he has received the parcel from me for you. I hope he manages to deliver it alright.

No, Darling, I have no address from the soldiers at the railway so I shall have to continue to send them via Len.

Mrs H's exploits are astounding me. I always thought her morals were slightly lacking, but I didn't think she was as bad as this. Still, we live and learn, do we not!

Now about me! After four weeks of idleness — including

463, Devon Mansions,
Tooley Street,
London, S.E.1.

2nd May, 1946

My darling Astrid,

My Father handed me in bed yesterday morning your letter of the 7th of April sent via the civilian post. It took a long time to get here, as you can see, but it did arrive, and that is something.

The mystery of my missing letters has apparently been cleared up now. Len tells me he had some returned to him and one he forwarded has actually been lost. However, let us hope no more will go astray. Until I hear that you have received those I forwarded through the civilian post, though, I will continue to write to Len and let him forward my letters to you. This would appear to be the safest way at the moment.

Well, dear, I have received no reply from the Authorities in London so I shall be going to see them as soon as I can get time off from Work. Also, I am going to write to the Welfare Officer of 13 Corps H!Q. in Germany and perhaps this may result in something tangible. This waiting for you is getting me nowhere – we are all waiting to see you come to England!!

I have not heard from George at all. Of course, you know that he lives a very long way from me indeed so it would have to be a very special occasion before I could go to see him. I did write to him once but received no reply. Perhaps one of these days we shall all meet again, eh?

Last night I went to a Hall in London where our Regiment used to meet before the War, and saw a lot of the Chaps who are now finished with the Army and back in civilian life. Do you remember Norman who used to work in the Office with Ilse? He came to my house in a car and we went to the meeting in that. Naturally a lot of BEER was drunk and this morning I had a very bad headache. You have seen me before with bad headaches, have not you?

Well, Darling, this is about all I can think of at the moment, so I will go now to bed to dream of you. Please do not worry, everything will turn out alright in the end.

With all my love and very best
wishes,
Yours as always,

Bert xxxxxxxxxx

Very best wishes and regards from my Mother and Father.
If you get time perhaps you could write to them, eh?

463 Devon Mansions,
Tooley St.,
London, S.E.1.

Monday 6 May 46.

Astrid Dear!

On Saturday last I received through the civilian post your letter dated 7 April. As you can see this way it takes about a month for your letters to reach me. I think it would be better for you to send yours through Œ Jen or some other soldier for quickness, don't you?

I have sent you some letters through the civilian post, but I hope they reach you in quicker time than a month.

Have you received the letters yet where I have sent the official one for you to show to the British Consul or Authorities there? I have heard from the Authorities in London and they say this method is quite right but it will take some time for you to get here owing to the limited transport facilities. Directly you get those letters stating I want to marry you, Darling, I think you had best ask advice at UNRRA or the British Military Government. They should know something about it. I have also written to the Welfare Officer at the Headquarters in Germany and perhaps this too will quicken things.

Well, dear, I do not do much these days, except think of you. I rarely go out at night, nearly always stopping in to play cards with my Mother and Father.

Last Friday I went to the dogs (do you remember what this is?) but we never won much money! And I have written after a new job, so wish me luck.

Well, Darling, it is time I went to bed, so here is wishing you all the best.

All my love and ~~too~~ lots of kisses,
Bert.
xxx xxvxvx

Best regards from my Ma & Pa.

463 Devon Mansions,
Tooley St,
London, S.E.1.

Sunday 12 May 46.

Darling,

Thank you very much indeed for your letters. The one you sent by Len came yesterday, and the one you sent by civilian post on the 4 April came the day before, so you see the quickest way for you to send your mail is through Len or some other soldier. It seems, though, that the best way for me to send you letters is through the civilian post so I shall do that and hope for the best.

I am especially pleased that you received the letter addressed to the Railway Office because that was most important. I have heard from the Home Office who say that what I have done so far is correct, but travelling facilities (that is the Railway, and Autos, etc) are so limited in Germany that the matter cannot be hurried. However, Dear, you must keep on to the Authorities there, that is the best way. I have already written to the Welfare Officer at B Corps HQ. and if I hear anything from him I will let you know.

How is your eye? You had better not do any more wood hacking — let that old cow Holthaus do it!!

I was sorry to hear that you had to part with Vernons but I suppose it was a bit awkward for you to keep. Have you heard from Willi as to how she is going on — any Kint yet?

Tonight I have been to the dog racing with my friend but we did not win any money. Perhaps we shall another time.

Well, Darling, I must go to bed now. So cheerio till the next time. Keep smiling perhaps it will not be so long before we meet again.

3.

Yours as always,

All my love,

Bert

xxxxxxxxx
(extra special big
ones this time!).

P.S. Ma and Pa send their best regards.

Mr. A. J. Wallis,
463 Devon Mansions,
Tooley St,
London, S.E.1.

Monday 20th May 1946.

My Darling Astrid,

Thank you very much indeed for your letters.

I am a stupid idiot — the father of all idiots (remember?) Do you remember me writing to you and saying that I had sent a letter to the military authorities in Germany? Well this has been returned to me — I put "13 Corps HQ" instead of "30 Corps HQ". However, I am re-addressing the letter and perhaps it will then get to the right people.

Have you managed to see anybody in Authority yet? It seems a pity that I am not there to help you, but you must try and get to the right people. Darling. I shall keep a good look out for that English soldier you mention. It was very good of him to offer to lend you the money — please thank him for me.

Just in case it may be of assistance to you I am sending with this letter the letter I received from the Home Office.

How is your eye, my silly one — I sincerely hope it is better now. Don't forget, no more "holtz-hacken" (is that correct?).

Today I went after a new job. The money is more and the number of hours to work per week are less, so I hope I get it. I shall know tomorrow.

Well, Darling, my bed-time is here, so here's to the next time. Hurry up now and get that permission to come to England.

With very best wishes and <u>all</u> my love,

Yours as ever,

Bert.

P.S. Best regards from Ma & Pa!

463, Devon Mansions,
Tooley Street,
London, S.E.1.

Tuesday, 4th June, 1946

My Dear Astrid,

Thank you for your letter of the 28th May received today.

From your last letter I thought that everything was going splendidly but now you have got me worried again. Government, especially Military Government, Departments are famous for their longwindedness so I suppose I was too pessimistic in hoping that you would soon be in England. However, I have written to the two addresses you gave and perhaps this will quicken things up a bit.

You may, or may not, be sorry to learn that so far I have not yet changed my jobs, but I am still trying and have not yet given up hope. You know why I want another job, don't you? So that I can earn more money for when you do arrive in England.

Have you managed to go to see Vernons yet, Darling? Needless to say I am very interested in her and her little dogs. I wish I were nearer then perhaps I could have (Imean "we") one of her off-spring.

The weather here is "sow-wedder"!!! Not a bit like it should be in June. Have you managed to go down by the canal lately to get brown?

I still have not heard from George. One of these days when I think of it I will write him again and perhaps this will bring forth a letter from him.

Well, Darling, it is again time I went to the land of slumber - that means sleep - so I will say cheerio once more.

All my love and very best wishes,

Yours as ever,
Bert
xxxxxxxx

P!S! Kindest regards from my Mother and Father.

A. J. Wallis
463 Devon Mansions,
Tooley St.,
London, S.E.1.

Monday, 17 June 46.

My dear Astrid,

Thank you very much indeed for your letter of the 13th June. I am glad that at last I have another soldier's address to write to, because this is a much quicker way than the civilian post.

I have written to Miss Kennedy and the Passport Office. I did this quite a time ago and sent you copies of the letters I wrote. Perhaps you will have received them by the time you get this letter. I have heard from the Passport Office and I must now write to them again sending letters from my Employer and a Clergyman and from my landlord saying that I am able to marry you and can support you. So you see perhaps it will not be too long now before we see one another again.

I am sorry to hear that you are so thin now, Sweetheart. But once you get here we will soon fatten you up again.

And I am very sorry to hear about poor old Vernono. I hope she soon gets well again.

Len is now in England. I have not seen him yet but no doubt we will soon arrange a meeting.

Well, Darling, this is all the note-paper we have in the house so I will have to close now, but I will write again tomorrow or the next day.

Cheerio for now, Sweetheart, please do not worry too much. All my love and very best wishes,

Bert.
xxxxxx

Best regards from Ma + Pa. And please thank Jock Brodie for me — I would have written him a note but

463, Devon Mansions,
Tooley Street,
London, S.E.1.

Monday, 24th June, 1946

My Darling Astrid,

Last week I had about four letters from you so you can see I was a very lucky man.

Believe me I am very worried about you because I can realise what travelling on the Railways in Germany must entail and I can only hope that you will not have to endure all this time on trains much longer. It certainly seems a very difficult business getting a passport, but I have had a letter from Miss Kennedy and she thinks everything will be alright once you have been before the doctor. I am counting the days, Dear.

The reason why I am always just going to sleep in my letters is very easily explained. You see, I cannot write them at work - I am too busy there - and when I come home and have my meal I like to sit for a while and rest (and you know how I like sitting - I don't always fall asleep though) and when eventually I write letters to you it is always about 10.30 p.m. or perhaps later. See!!!!!!

My Mother has received your letter and is going to reply to this shortly. Today (this morning) I told her what you wanted so she bought some coffee, cocoa, chocolate, cigarettes and skin food. These I will send off tomorrow or the next day to L/Cpl Paynter. You must not let XX Mrs. H. have too much though, Darling, even if it means opening the parcel at the Railway Station and hiding the stuff. After what you have written me about her I do not like her. But if you tell her I send good wishes this might make her be nicer to you - what do you think?

Since you ask, Cooke, your writing is very good indeed and I have no trouble at all in reading your letters. Can

you speak it as good as you can write English? I hope
so. You mention in your small list of requirements
"two package of black colour" - I think you mean the
dyes for clothes so I am sending two of these.

Well, Darling, my head is emptier than empty so
ONCE AGAIN it is time for me to go to SLUMBERLAND - hope
that does not make you annoyed.

Cheerio for now, then, very best wishes and
ALL my love,

*Bert*
xxxxxxxxx


Best wishes and kindest regards to Fr. Holthaus. Hope
she is keeping well.

A. J. Wallis,
463 Devon Mansions,
Tooley St.,
London, S.E.1.

Tuesday 2nd July, 1946

Patricia Darling,

I really meant to write you a long letter tonight when I reached home from my work, but just as I finished my meal a knock came to the door and when we opened the door there was my cousin and her husband who had just finished with the Army. So you can imagine that as I have not seen him for 4½ years a little celebration was called for so we went to the beer-house and had quite a drop to drink!!! The time is now past midnight so you can guess what with the beer and my work I am ready for slumberland (I hope that word doesn't make you too mad!).

2

Well, Dear. Last week I sent off the few things you asked for and I hope they arrive safely. My Mother sent you the chocolate.

I note that your money is nearly all gone and needless to say I am very worried. I wrote to Miss Kennedy and asked her whether the cost of your passage home here could be paid by me, but so far I haven't received any reply. If you need any at the moment, Darling, ask h/Cpl Paynter for what you want then tell me his address in England and I will send the equivalent there — if you cannot understand this quite show it to h/Cpl Paynter and he will be willing to help, I am sure. You see, we are not allowed to send money out of England to Germany.

3.

well, Dear, my head is going round and round !! (I hope you can understand my writing). So I must away to bed. More tomorrow or the next day.

    Yours as ever,

      All my love and very best wishes,

        Bert.

P.S. Best regards from Mum & Dad.

463, Devon Mansions,
Tooley Street,
London, S.E.1.

Sunday, 21st July 1946.

Astrid Darling,

What has happened to the mail. All last week I was waiting for a letter from you but none appeared. I am really sorry I have not written before because now I realise you are probably travelling on that old railway again. Please write soon, Dear!

I have had a letter from Miss Kennedy. You probably know - she herself is now married; I must write and wish her luck. She says that it could probably be arranged for you to travel to England and the cost be paid by me to the London office of the Association with which she is connected. This money matter is really a source of worry to me Darling. How are you managing? Please do write and tell me the truth. If you are wanting at all I must send some to Miss Kennedy for you.

Did you get the letter my Mother sent to you? I don't think you could have done because I am sure you would have written.

I have not seen Len since he was discharged from the Army, but that is probably my fault. I have not replied to the last letter he sent me and that was over a month ago - so you can see I am still very slow at corresponding.

Last night I went to the Licht Spiel (Kinema to you, Darling) on my own - that is the first time I have been to British Pictures since 1942. I am getting good, you see, while I am at the Pictures I am not drinking beer and too much beer makes me fat.

Tonight I went with my Mother and Father for some beer but this is very short in England at the present time so I did not have a lot - do I hear you say that is good for me?

    I do not look for a new job any more. I think it is best for me to wait until you are home. You see, when you get here I shall want some time off and if I get a different job perhaps this would be difficult. So hurry up and come home, please!!!!!!!

    Well, Darling, this is not much of a letter, I know, but I promise you I shall write again in a day or so. Till then keep smiling.

                      Very best wishes and ALL my love,

                        Yours as always,

                          *Bert*
                     xxxxxxxxxxxx
                     xxxxxxxxxxx
                      (all for you!)

Very best wishes from Ma and Pa.

*Regards to H. Holthous*

463, Devon Mansions,
Tooley Street,
LONDON, S.E.1.

1st August, 1946

Astrid Darling,

Yet another week has gone by without any news from you. What has happened out there?

Last Sunday Len came down to London from Birmingham. He too has not heard from Ilse and he came to learn whether I had heard from you. We are wondering whether the Cpl Paynter to whom we have been addressing our letters has gone from Vorsfelde.

Well, Dear, the weather here is very nice in parts. If we were still at Lauterberg we would be going for nice walks, or horse riding, wouldn't we. They were very nice days indeed - perhaps we have something to thank the war for after all.

Next weekend is holiday weekend but the trains and autobuses are too packed to go anywhere. I think I shall stay at home - and DRINK. I know you will not believe me but I have very little beer these days. Perhaps on Saturdays I drink a little and on Sundays too, but never hardly during the week. You see, I am reforming!!!

It surely should be time now that you should be coming over. I cannot understand why it is taking so long and soon I shall write again to the Passport Office.

Have you heard from Fanny recently? I have not had any news from George at all, but I should imagine he is getting on alright.

Well, Darling, my head is again empty (as always) so I must away to do some work. Cheerio until the next time then.

Very best wishes,

and A L L my love,

Bert.
XXXXXXXXXXXXXXX

P.S. Very best regards from Ma and Pa (did you ever receive my Mother's letter).

463, Devon Mansions,
Tooley Street,
London, S.E.1.

11th August, 1946

Darling Astrid,

Last Saturday I received the first letter from zou for about four weeks, and indeed I also notice that you have received no mail from me. I can't understand this because I have written you at least once per week - probably it is because the L/Cpl moved from Vorsfelde. I am taking a chance now and sending this letter to the Sgt that Ilse has 'caught' and I sincerely hope it reaches you.

I was very pleased to learn from your letter that Vernons after all was alright - what is the matter with that old cow Holthaus? Why does she want to tell so many lies?

Is the Camp you are going to at Brunswick a step on the way home? You say it is a mixed Nationalities Camp so I am hoping this is so. If I do not hear from you again for so long I will write to the Miss Kennedy - perhaps this would be a way to get some news.

Last week was August holiday in England and I went to Len's home in Birmingham for three days. We had a very good time - went to the horse races. The horses reminded me of Lauterberg - do you remember our horse rides? And what a pair of jockeys were Fanay and George!!!!

At work they keep on asking me when am I going to take my holidays - I get two weeks - but of course I am waiting for you so that we can leave London for this time together. Hurry up Darling and get to England!!!!

Well, Sweetheart, my head is again empty so until tomorrow I will say cheerio. Try and keep smiling, it will not be long now before we see one another.

Very best wishes and A L L my love,

Yours as ever,

Bert
xxxxxxxxxxxx
xxxxxxxxx

Best regards from Ma and Pa.

463, Devon Mansions,
Tooley Street,
London, S.E.1.

Friday, 16th August, 1946

Darling Astrid,

On my return from work today your letter of the 11th August was waiting for me. Believe me Dear I am as concerned as you about the delay and I am writing tonight to the Passport Control Officer, Lubbecke, and if I can get no satisfaction from this source then I am going to write to my Member of Parliament in England. The time is certainly dragging on and I am beginning to get impatient.

Today is "sow-wedder" in England. Plenty of rain and no sunshine. Very good for the ducks - understand?

Is Ilse still at Vorsfelde too? You do not state in your letter - it will make me even more mad if she gets away from Germany before you Darling!

At work every day they are asking me when shall I take my two weeks holidays, but I keep on saying later, later! I am waiting for you, Dear. I think perhaps it will not be too long now!!!

Well, Darling, I am going to write now to the Passport Officer, so I must say cheerio for now. Very best wishes and  A L L  my love,

Yours as ever,
Bert xxxxxxxx xxxxxxx
xx xxx xxx xxxx

(more to come, personally)

Very best wishes from my Ma and Pa!

463, Devon Mansions,
Tooley Street,
London, S.E.1.

Monday, 26th August, 1946

Astrid Darling,

On Saturday last there was such a big surprise waiting for me when I arrived home from my work. Your letter of 18th August was in the house for me and it was the best letter I have had yet because the photos of you are so good. You write that you think they are the best photos you have ever had done; this I cannot say, but they are certainly the best I have seen of you. You look very happy in them all which was a good thing to see. Ma thinks they are exceptionally good too. I like best the one of you on your own, then that with Ilse laying down in the grass and then that of you and Ilse standing together. I notice from the pictures that you have altered that brown frock you used to wear - did you do that yourself, Dear, or did you go to the tailors?

I am very worried now that you are at the Camp. I have written to the Passport Officer at Lubbecke but so far have not received any reply. Is Miss Kennedy at Brunswick still, Darling? Perhaps she can help to quicken matters for us.

Every day is the same - go to work and then come home, eat and to bed. I am certainly waiting for the day when you arrive in England. Hurry up!!!! I am getting tired of just dreaming of you - you must soon be by my side!

The weather in England this summer has been very bad indeed and the people are saying that perhaps September will be the best month for the sunshine. I am hoping so because I must in any case take my two weeks holidays in that month. I am hoping all the time that we will be together for this holiday - you must pray hard, Darling!!!

- 2 -

You know I am on my holidays this week and next
week and I really thought we were going to be able to
spend them together away from London.  We are certainly
a very lucky couple, aren't we.  But still, do not
despair, Darling, perhaps we shall see one another
sooner than we expect.

Well, Sweetheart, it is time I was getting this
letter posted if it is to reach you quickly, so I
will close now.   Please do not worry too much - I
am going to see everyone I can to get the matter quickened
from this end.

Cheerio for now then!  Very best wishes and
A L L  my love,

       Yours as always,

       Bert.

xxxxxxxxxxxxxx
xxxxxxxxxxxxx
      X *this is the one you are going to get when I see you first!*

P.S.   Kindest regards and very best wishes from
       Ma and Pa.

463; Devon Mansions,
Tooley Street,
London, S.E.1.

Thurs., 26th Sept. 46

Darling Astrid,

Today I received your letter and I think I must be the most disappointed man in England. Last Friday I got a letter from Mrs. Currie saying that you would probably be arriving this week and then on Saturday I received a telegram saying that you would arrive at Hull at 08.00 hrs on the 24th. I travelled all night on the train up to Hull and after waiting until everybody had got off the ship I realised that you had not travelled after all. I immediately saw the officer in charge who put a telephone call through to Germany to find out why you had not come and was told that you had been detained pending new embarkation instructions. Everyone here at home was waiting for me to return with the new Mrs. Wallis (Astrid) but I had to come back alone. Yesterday I left the house at nine o'clock in the morning and did not return until five o'clock in the evening; I had been to see if I could find out something definite about you because until I got your letter this morning I had no idea where you had been stopped. One gentleman promised to cable Brunswick and I have to telephone him this afternoon to find out what he has learned. If you are delayed much longer then I shall have to write to the Prime Minister of England about it. Something MUST be done very soon to bring us together again.

How are you going on for money, Dear. If you have none perhaps you could borrow some from the relief officer and I will send whatever the amount is to his home in England.

# MEDICAL CLEARANCE CERTIFICATE

| 1st | | 2nd | | | | | |
|---|---|---|---|---|---|---|---|
| L | I. | L | I. | L | I. | L | I. |
| D.D.T. | | AL & M. KJ | | HEAT. | | OTHER | |

(25) Dates of Disinfestation

(26) PHYSICAL CONDITION ON ARRIVAL

| L | M. | | C.D. | | D. | |

REMARKS

(27) IMMUNIZATION RECORD

| Types | Dose | Date | Initials |
|---|---|---|---|
| T (Epid) | 1. | 10.11.49 | |
| | 2. | 18.11.49 | |
| | 3. | 3.12.46 | |
| D. | 1. | | |
| | 2. | | |
| T.T. (Tab.) | 1. | 14.v. | 0.3% |
| | 2. | 28.v. | 1.0 |
| | 3. | | |
| O. | | | |
| S. Vacc. Read. | | | Reaction L. V. VA. |

(28) Final Medical Inspection: F.F.I.
M.L.R.M.  Date 30th Mar 24  M.R.
Medical Examiner

(30) RECEPTION CENTER RECORD

Arrival Medical Inspection -:
Date
Medical Examiner

(29) MOVEMENT AUTHORIZATION OR VISA

---

(31) SUPPLEMENTARY RECORD

Temporary Identity Certificate Issued —:

| | Number | Date | Signature of Authority |
|---|---|---|---|
| Depart for England | | 20/3/48 | |

Duplicate

# A.E.F. D.P. REGISTRATION RECORD

**(1) Registration No.** G 22-67784.

Original ☑  Duplicate ☑

| A | B | C | D | E | F | G | H | I | J |
|---|---|---|---|---|---|---|---|---|---|
| | | | | |1|1|3| | |

For coding purposes

**(2) Family Name** Härm **Other Given Names** Astrid.

**(3)** Single ☐ Married ☐ M ☐
Widowed ☐ Divorced ☐ F ☑
**(4) Marital Status** **(5) Sex**

**(6) Birthdate** 25.4.1924 **Birthplace** Dorpat. **Province** Estonia. **Country** **(6) Claimed Nationality** Estonian.

**(9) Number of Dependents:** — **(7) Religion (Optional)** Protestant **(8) Number of Accompanying Family Members:** —

**(10) Full Name of Father** Johannes. **(11) Full Maiden Name of Mother** Karu Lydia.

**(12) Desired Destination** London England. **(13) Last Permanent Residence or Residence January 1, 1938.** Fellin. Fellin. Estonia.
City or Village  Province  Country  City or Village  Province  Country

**(14) Usual Trade, Occupation or Profession** High School. **(15) Performed in What Kind of Establishment** **(16) Other Trades or Occupations**

**(17) Languages Spoken in Order of Fluency** a. Estonian, b. English, c. German. **(18) Do You Claim to be a Prisoner of War** Yes ☐ No ☑

**(20) Signature of Registrant:** Astrid Härm **(21) Signature of Registrar:** **(19) Amount and Kind of Currency in your Possession** —

**(22) Destination or Reception Center:** **Date:** 8.12.45 **Assembly Center No.** 2925

| (23) Code for Issue | 1 | 2 | 3 | 4 | 5 | 6 | 7 | 8 | 9 | 10 | 11 | 12 | 13 | 14 | 15 | 16 | 17 | 18 | 19 | 20 | 21 | 22 | 23 | 24 | 25 | 26 | 27 | 28 |
|---|---|---|---|---|---|---|---|---|---|---|---|---|---|---|---|---|---|---|---|---|---|---|---|---|---|---|---|---|
| | | | | | | | | | | | | | | | | | | | | | | | | | | | | |

Name or Number  City or Village  Province  Country

**(24) Remarks**

DP-2

Mum and Dad on the German Gun Carriage Horses

Broadstairs before they were married

Bude, Cornwall 1954 (taken by me)

# GROWING UP

I certainly did not notice anything unusual or different about my mother when I was growing up. I think I did wonder why I only had one set of grandparents when everyone else had two, but I was too young to think much about it. I had a wonderful childhood and from an early age was around dogs and horses whenever I could be. I used to walk eight miles at the age of ten, if Dad could not take me, to the farm where I went riding.

I could never understand where I got my love of horses and riding. Dad was born in Bermondsey, went to grammar school there and the closest he came to riding horses was riding a bicycle although of course later I was to find out about his riding with my mother in Germany.

Dad always did the football pools (Vernons) and always promised me that if he ever won them he would buy me a pony. Well, as luck would have it, one Saturday poor Dad did win the pools. Unfortunately, that week there were so many draws that the first prize was not very much and he won just over £100. I was twelve at the time and of course would not let the matter drop.

"Oh Dad, you *promised* me that if you ever won the pools you would buy me a pony. Dad you promised!"

Of course, dear Dad bought me a pony – called Music – with a saddle and bridle for £90 in 1962 and he only had enough left for a transistor radio (a Dansette) that he bought for himself, and which I also commandeered to listen to Radio Luxemburg.

I shall never forget going to Princes Risborough to see Music. Dad had found someone who lived seven miles away who could keep a pony for us, and she had told him about Music. Well, I took her out on the main road, started to canter up the grass verge and to my horror I couldn't stop. I did the only thing that I could think of and turned her into the hedge. Music was a thoroughbred pony and so was a bit wound up by this, so I thought that it would probably be safer to lead her back to the establishment rather than ride her. Of course, everyone was worried about what had happened to me, and breathed a sigh of relief when I finally showed up, but then proceeded, to my horror, to discuss with Mum and Dad the fact that they did not think I should have the pony as I could not control it. Well, that was like a red rag to a bull, and in retrospect I think my grandfather's spirit must have reared its head because I was determined to have Music there and then. Mum and Dad, knowing how stubborn I could be, relented and I had my first wonderful pony. Music was sold to us as seven years old but later we were to find out that she was probably nearer twenty. She was a complete nutcase, but she certainly taught me how to ride.

I had to prove that I wanted my pony and help pay for her keep, so I used to get up at 5.30am every morning, walk downhill for a mile and a half to the paper shop with my Alsatian, Rin Tin Tin, pick up the heavy papers for my paper-round and walk back to deliver the papers around the estate. I used to dread Thursday as it was local paper and Radio Times day and was an absolute killer! Rinty always used to cheat and when we passed our bungalow, he used to leave me to deliver the rest on my own! All this for the princely sum of ten shillings per week (or 50p in today's money). Because I did this, any extras that needed to be paid for, such as shoeing Music, for example, Dad very kindly paid for – but at least I was contributing a little and proving that I wanted the pony and did not just expect my parents to keep her for me, which to be honest, he could well have afforded to do. I am glad about this, because at least I learnt about the worth of things at an early age.

Music was first kept at Chartridge just outside of Chesham where I lived, and I used to walk from home to the Broadway, catch a bus and go and see her and then ride her. Later, Dad would collect me and I would do my schoolwork when I got home. I could not do this every day as the buses were infrequent and sometimes Dad did not get home until very late and it was too far to walk.

The lady, who we rented the field from, where we kept Music, was a bus conductor and lived in a caravan on a plot of land down a long lane. It was the only place that Dad could find at the time to keep a pony. I did not like it there very much. She had a lovely Alsatian that was chained up and not fed very well and so I used to always take dog food and biscuits when I visited. The lady was very rarely there and always left me notes on who to feed or when to stable Jim, her lovely big dun Thoroughbred horse. I didn't mind doing it, but I didn't think that her animals were very well looked after either.

On one occasion, she rode to the blacksmith with me, which was a long way away in Bovingdon, and when we got there, she informed me that she was going to catch a bus that came through to go work! She even had the nerve to ask if would I take her horse back to the stables. Me, a twelve-year-old! Of course I did it, riding Music and leading Jim back through miles of traffic.

The last straw came when I arrived one morning and she had left a note for me to feed Jim. I gaily picked up the bucket with his feed and went to the stable, and, horror of horrors, he was lying there dead. It broke my heart. There was such an awful look on his face and his lips were pulled back and it looked like he had died in agony – from what, I have no idea, maybe colic – but that picture will live with me forever. I ran to the nearest phone box (no mobiles in those days) and luckily I had some coins that I could use and phoned the bus station in Amersham where she worked, and left a message to tell her what had happened. Although I can still see her face, I cannot for the life of me remember her name. Perhaps that is just as well!

Dad found me another farm in Amersham to keep Music – I don't know how – but it was so good as a lot of other people kept horses there too, and so I had company on occasion when I went riding, although I still loved riding on my own, just me and my pony. What joy.

The costs at Clarks Farm, where Music was kept, were fifteen shillings per week in the summer and thirty shillings per week in the winter, which included a milk churn full of rolled oats. Music lived out all year and back then in the sixties in Buckinghamshire, the weather seemed to be a lot better. Not so much rain, and also the ground was porous chalk and so did not really get that muddy either.

## Estonia and Equines

I really had the bug and used to walk to see her from school every night of the week. In the summer I could ride and Dad would collect me on his way home from work in the city and then I would do my homework. In the winter I would walk to see her and then walk home five miles in the dark because it would be too long to wait for Dad and then to do my homework. I went to a lot of shows, and enjoyed show-jumping with my pony. Sometimes I hacked to shows as far as twelve miles away (poor Music) and sometimes we were lucky enough to be taken in a horsebox. I felt really grown up when I went with the BSJA (British Show Jumping Association) people to St Albans and won lots of rosettes. I was only 14, so not even old enough to join a riding club, but I loved it so much.

Dad even scraped together and bought me another horse so that I had two to take show jumping. By this time I had done my GCEs in Year 5 at Little Chalfont High School for Girls. I started off at Dr Challoner's Grammar School which had been co-educational, but had been split after Year 3 and so then I had to move to Little Chalfont High School for Girls – but I was happy with this, as it was closer to my beloved pony. When I left school, I began working at the Equity & Law Head Office in High Wycombe. My only career information had been an interview with Miss McMaster the Headmistress of Little Chalfont High School for Girls, which went, and I quote: "…and what do you want to do when you leave School?" I said "Work with horses," to which I got a horrified look, and she replied, "Oh, there's no money in that – you will have to think of something else." That was it! Dismissed!

# WONDERING

All this time, I never questioned Mum's background – to me, she did not seem different in any way to anyone else's Mum. Nobody had heard of Estonia and nobody spoke about Estonia at home. Now I think about it, perhaps it was because Mum was terrified that someone would find out that she was in England and order her back to Estonia and her awful memories. That is something I have found in life; you always remember things as you last knew them to be. To live with those memories must have been awful for Mum.

The only thing that I did notice was that Mum would put words a different way round in a sentence (and having since learnt Estonian I can quite see why). She would also pronounce some words differently until she knew the correct pronunciation, but I always thought that she was just fooling around. For example, 'sausage' she would pronounce as 'sow-sa-ga'. She was always very good at languages at school and was in fact going on to University in Tartu before the country was invaded yet again.

When I was four or five, she worked part-time in an office in the company that Dad was Sales Director

## Estonia and Equines

for. It must have been quite daunting but she learnt a lot of her English there. When we moved from Ealing to Buckinghamshire when I was 8 years old, she worked part time in the accounts office for Van Houten, the big chocolate and sweet company (which was great because we always had lots of sweets and chocolate at home!) People that met my mother used to think that she had an accent, but I never noticed it as I suppose it was just normal to me.

I also never asked her about her previous life. Mainly, I think, because after asking her once she ended up in tears and intuitively I understood that she never really wanted to talk about it

I first starting wondering about my Estonian ancestors with the advent of the Internet and computers, as I thought perhaps it would make it a lot easier to find out about my heritage. In 2000, I was made redundant after working for a company for twenty-nine years and it was after this happened and I had some spare time, that I first bought my own computer. I emailed the records office in Tallinn and gave them all the information that I had about our family. I never had a reply. I was very disappointed and really did not think a lot more about it, as I did not know which way to go after that. I couldn't ask Mum, not that she would have had any more idea than me. Estonia had still not really burst on to the scene so to speak and so that was that; I had to live with my disappointment and thought that I would never be able to find out anything more than I already knew.

# SEARCHING

My mother started to get ill with dementia around 2002. In 2000 she went into hospital to have a hip replacement and after the operation they could not get her temperature back up to proper levels. She walked with crutches afterwards for the rest of her life. She had her other hip replaced in September 2001, which went very well, but still she never discarded the crutches, no matter how hard we tried to cajole her. I think this contributed to her dementia. The anaesthetic and the awful horrors that she had suffered in her formative years can't have helped either.

Back in the late 1970s I thought it would be nice if I could take Mum back to her homeland and looked at how to go about getting her there. Well, the nearest I could do was a boat trip that called into the port at Tallinn for one day. To do this I had to get a visa from the Russian Embassy and once again I hit a wall. That was the end of it. Mum did not want me to try as (and I now understand her concerns) she thought that if she went there they would find out somehow that she had fled in 1946 and keep her there against her will. So I booked a holiday in Austria for Mum and Dad instead. This

## Estonia and Equines

was the first time that she had left England since she came as a refugee in 1946 and also the nearest she could get to her beloved Estonia. When she returned she did indeed say that some of the countryside was very similar. For the next few years when they went away it was to places like Ibiza, Majorca and then they soon started going for four or five months through the winter. And so time went on.

I lived in Langtree when we got married, and we were there for twelve years. When we left Langtree, we moved to Little Collingsdown and Mum and Dad came and lived next-door to us, in 1984. Dad was 69 and Mum was 60. My friend's husband was the European Manager of a big engineering company and he went on a trip to Estonia. I can't remember which year but it was probably when Estonia had just started coming into the market for cheap labour, so I guess it was around 1995-6. He very kindly brought back some newspapers and maps for Mum. She loved looking at the papers and maps and showing me where she was born, where they lived and the capital Tallinn, but could not understand any of the language. Understandable I suppose, as she had not spoken her native language for fifty years, by this time. It's hard to believe that the Soviet Union only recognised the independence of Estonia on 6th September 1991 and from then the last Russian troops left on 31st August 1994.

Dad's health had also been failing for some time and as Mum's dementia had been getting daily worse, I'm sure that her health problems contributed to Dad's own failing health. I went home from work one particular lunchtime to take Dad to the doctor for a routine appointment. He asked me to go in with him, which I did, although he seemed quite cheerful and said that he was glad to get out for a while, even if it was only a drive in the country to the doctor. I started to be a bit worried as the doctor put Dad behind screens and took a long while to examine him and was 'umming' and 'ahhing'. The doctor told Dad that he was 99% sure that he had an aneurism and that he ought to go to hospital and have something done about it before it burst. But Dad, who was 92 at the time said no, and that he had had a really good 'innings' (as he put it) and did not want to be messed around with. He said he would take whatever live threw at him.

Dad left the surgery, but the doctor called me back and said that he thought the aneurism was quite bad and that it could burst in two months or two years, but to warn me that when it did there was no way that an ambulance crew would get to him in time, and that it would take around twenty minutes and he would die in agony. I'm sure he told me this to prepare me for the worst, though I sincerely hoped that somehow it would not come to that. Dad did not know what the doctor had told me and it was something that I would have to live with, as I was not going to breathe a word to Dad.

Well, as it happened, we got home and Dad got out of the car and went to go up the steps to his home. I went round the side of the 4 x 4 to help Mum out. It was then that Dad shouted to me to come and help him. He had fallen over. Unbeknownst to me he had ischemic heart disease and blood was not getting to his extremities, and he had no feeling in his legs. I left Mum, rushed over and with some difficulty picked him up and got him inside. He was a bit shaken, but seemed none the worse for his tumble. I then went and helped Mum out of the car and indoors, made them both a cup of tea and got lunch together. By the time I had to go back to work, Dad seemed to have recovered!

## Estonia and Equines

I got home at around 5.30pm and Ron and I went straight over to sit with Mum and Dad and have a cup of tea and get their food for them. Dad seemed really cheerful then and I am so glad because that is the last picture that I have of him in my head.

It was around 10.00pm that Mum came struggling in to say that she wanted to go to bed, but she couldn't as 'he' was lying across the bed and she could get into it. My blood ran cold and I ran and got Ron. We both went across to Mum's home. I stayed in the lounge with Mum and Ron went to the bedroom. My worst fears were realised and Ron came out and said that he thought that father had passed away. I ran back over to our house and rang for an ambulance and told them what had happened. The paramedic came, and Ron went with him and they did whatever they did. I stayed out with Mum. The paramedic rang the police and then they came and questioned us, and then they rang for the undertaker. What a night. I think the undertaker arrived at around 3.00am. The only good thing was that Mum's dementia stopped her from realising exactly what had happened. She sat there and as the undertakers were taking Dad away she looked to me and said, "Are they taking my husband?" I replied, "Yes, Mum, and my father."

She only mentioned Dad once more after that: about two days later, when I was sitting with her she fell asleep, and when she awoke, she jumped and looked at me as if she had seen a ghost. I asked her if she was all right, and she said that she thought I was 'Bert' (Dad) and that was the last time she mentioned him.

I then had a big decision to make. Did I or did I not take Mum to Dad's funeral? I thought about it long and hard, but her dementia had got really bad and she kept repeating the same thing over and over again, and as she had not mentioned him at all, I thought that it would probably be kinder for her and for me if I didn't mention the funeral. It obviously did not occur to her that there would be one and that it was final when they took Dad away. I have thought about it afterwards and part of me feels guilty, but Mum wasn't Mum anymore and I cling to that fact on the dark days when I do feel guilty.

On the day of the funeral, Ron parked his van outside in the road so that it could not been seen and we told Mum that we were going out for a couple of hours. At this time she was still just well enough to be left on her own in the warm room with the TV on and her cat Mabel on her lap. They would both sit like that happily for hours. The one good thing (if you can call it a good thing) is that she had no inclination to get up and walk very far, as it was painful for her, so I never had the worry that she would go wandering about, and as long as she had the cat there purring on her lap she was fine.

As funerals go, it was a celebration of Dad's life, which everyone seemed to enjoy (if that is the right word). We had a humanist service (I only learnt of such a thing as a very dear friend of ours in Oxfordshire had passed away in December 2006 and although I was heartbroken, the service was wonderful and as Dad was not a religious person, and I had had no instruction, I could only do what I thought he would have liked) and so we celebrated his life. Having never done anything like that before, I hope I did him proud. I then had to choose music and so I racked my brains. When I was ten and until I was twelve I had piano lessons, as all little girls did, and Dad's two favourite pieces were the first movement of Beethoven's Moonlight Sonata and Für Elise, so I chose those pieces in that order.

## Estonia and Equines

The only relations that I had (which were obviously on Dad's side) came to the funeral. They consisted of Mary and Peter, who were the children of my Dad's eldest brother Tom. Both came down from London with their respective spouses, and Mary's daughter and her fiancé Scott. That was it. That was the sum total. My friends who knew Dad made up the rest of the contingent.

It was that day, Thursday 12th July 2007, that I decided I wanted to find the rest of my family that I had never known if indeed they existed.

# THE SEARCH FOR MY RELATIONS

I spent hours poring over the internet on my computer at home. All I had was my grandfather's name: Johannes Voldemar Till. In 2007 there was not that much on the Internet about Estonia and everything there was was in the Estonian language – so basically I was up the proverbial 'gum tree'. Anyhow, I was not going to be swayed from my task and so I kept at it. Then, I struck gold! A Museum of Occupation. It was all in Estonian but there it was – Johannes-Voldemar Till! Could there be more than one, I asked myself? How would I know it was my grandfather?

My next move on the Internet was to use a search engine to research how to find relatives in Estonia. There were several ways of doing it. Apparently, it could be done by yourself, but I thought this would prove to be very longwinded and virtually impossible because of the language barrier, and I was beginning to despair. My bright idea of finding relatives and thinking it would be easy with the advent of the Internet was beginning to dissipate.

## Estonia and Equines

Then I saw that the quickest way was to contact a solicitor in Estonia, as the digging around in archives was going to be difficult for me, not just because of the language barrier, but also because so many people had been displaced over the years. So, I decided to look on the Internet for a solicitor in Tallinn. I emailed the piece I had found to them and asked them if they could translate it for me and then find out if there were any living relatives. Here's the email I sent to them:

---

Dear Sirs

Further to my previous e-mail of today's date, I have just found my grandfather's name in the Museum of Occupation on the Internet. I hope that this helps you to help me as obviously I do not understand the language.

**TILL, Johannes-Voldemar, Jaan**, s. 12.10.1897 Viljandimaa Holstre v., kõrg.., raamatupidaja, **arr.** 02.07.41 Rakvere, Kunderi 12, erin. 31.03.42 §58-4, 58-10, 58-11; surmaotsus; kinnip-k. Permi obl. Ussollag, otsus täide viidud 08.05.42. EV major. Süüdistati ülestõusu ettevalmistamises laagris. [ar 9861-E]

## THE SEARCH FOR MY RELATIONS

```
Yours faithfully

Ann Neale
```

To my amazement, I had an email back very same day, 14th August

---

```
Dear Mrs Ann Neale,

Yes, we are able to trace your
relatives on the grounds of data
you have. The costs will be 2000
USD which you can transfer as
follows:

Acc no IBAN EE 8310 1005 xxxx xxxx
xx
of OÜ Välisoigusabi Advokaadiburoo
SEB EESTI ÜHISPANK
Tornimäe 2, Tallinn 15010 Estonia
SWIFT code EE UH ee 2X
The searches may take about 1-2
months after the payment has come
in here.

Yours truly

Ivo Mahhov
```

I was so excited when the next email arrived with an attachment and rushed to open it. I was very proud when

## Estonia and Equines

I read the translation and all became a bit clearer: my grandfather had been in the cavalry. (So *that's* where my horsey nature came from!) Then I got to the fingerprints and the picture of him with his shaven head and I just burst into tears. How could anybody do this to another human being? I cannot imagine what life must have been like in that concentration camp. He was obviously going to be executed anyway so I was so proud to read that it was for starting a rebellion in the camp. It certainly sounded like he did not just 'roll over' and give up.

What a shock. I was so elated and then I could hardly wait for the next email to come, which was the page from the church book on 27th August 2007. I was a bit disappointed as it was very difficult to read and didn't tell me if I had any living relations. So, I had to wait until the 17th September when I received a list with family details dating from my great-grandfather. It was wonderful when I got to the end of the letter to find that Mum's sister was still alive – but also very sad to know that she was suffering with dementia in the same way as Mum – and my mind was alive with all kinds of thoughts, like could I actually take her back to her homeland to see her sister again?

---

```
Dear Mrs Ann Neal

The file that is attached to the
email contains an old church book
and it shows the names and date
of birth of your grand-grand-
grandfather and his wife and
children under no 3.
```

## THE SEARCH FOR MY RELATIONS

It would help us if you knew if
your aunt Margarite (Maret) and
uncle Alun (Allan) also left from
Estonia with your mother and if
they had any children your mother
knew about?

Many thanks,

Ivo Mahhov

Kairi Reiman

---

Dear Ivo Mahhov and Kairi Reiman

Thank you for the e-mail and
attached file. Unfortunately my
mother has senile dementia and does
not now remember having a brother
and a sister. The only thing that
she told me, years ago, was that
she left Estonia and fled to Germany
to stay with a German relation.

I do not know how old she was. All
I do know is that she was supposed
to go to University in Tartu, but
when the occupation began, she was
sent to Germany. I guess it was
after 1942 as she knew that her

> father had been arrested. I also
> recall she told me that her brother
> Allan has skied across the frozen
> sea to Finland. From what I could
> gather she did not know what had
> happened to her mother, brother and
> sister after she left Estonia. She
> came to England from Germany in
> 1946.
>
> So, I am sorry, but I am not much
> help.
>
> Kind regards
>
> Ann Neale

So, then I waited...

A letter arrived from Estonia together with photographs of Maret, Allan, my Uncle Dima, Marian (Maret and Dima's daughter) and her husband, Jaak, and their two children, Aarne and Erik. I wrote back immediately. I then looked up everything that I could about Estonia on the Internet. It looked very foreboding and certainly not like the land that Mum had described in her more lucid moments. There was lots of correspondence by letter with Dima and email with Marian, and exchanged presents at Christmas, and in the New Year I booked our flights to Estonia for 4th May, 2008.

Mum's brother Allan had emigrated to Australia with his mother (my grandmother) in many years before. Dima and Marian had only just managed to make contact with

Allan but unfortunately he was dying from cancer. He did manage to make a visit to his homeland after all those years just before he died on 25th July 2001 (which is spookily the date that Ron and I married in 1970), but poor Mum never did.

It was also a big shock for Marian and Dima. Suddenly out of the blue they learn that someone who they had presumed was dead and gone forever, was alive in England. I found out that they had contacted the only people they could think of, which was the Red Cross, to see if they had any information about Mum. Of course Mum left in such a hurry and I don't suppose she had a passport and that to all intents and purposes there was simply no record of her; she just disappeared off the face of the earth, and that, they thought, was that.

# FIRST VISIT

There are not many ways to fly direct to Estonia. The only options at that time were Estonian Air from Heathrow and Easyjet from Stansted. Our problem was that we live in the west-country and it was such a long way to either Heahtrow or Stansted. My cousin Marian suggested that it was probably better to fly Easyjet as Estonian air did not have a very good reputation for being on time.

We did not want to drive up to Stansted and so I saw that there were flights from Newquay in Cornwall to Stansted with Ryanair, starting at 99p. "Just the job," I thought. Well, I did book the flights but as in most cases the final cost of each ticket was £99 after extras like checking in, luggage etc.

Finally, the morning of 3rd May arrived and we had a taxi collect us early in the morning to take us to Newquay Airport. I was a complete bag of nerves (mainly because I hate flying) and also with some trepidation because I was on a journey of a lifetime. I never in my wildest dreams thought I would take a trip 60-years-old to Estonia, a place that seemed to have been forgotten in the mists of time until the Estonian began their peaceful struggle for independence. In fact, when

FIRST VISIT

anyone asked where I was going and I told them, they all said, "Where's that?"

We were flying to Stansted the day before our inaugural journey. The flight went well and then we transferred to the Best Western Hotel to await our flight to Estonia. We enjoyed a very nice lunch and a meal in the evening and requested an early morning call as the plane was leaving at 7.30 and we had to be at the airport and checked in by 5.30. Nerves and excitement were getting the better of me.

Once at the airport, we checked-in and went through all the normal security checks, boarded the plane and finally taxied down the runway and took off for Tallinn. The weather was very kind to us and we had a smooth flight. For once, my husband stayed awake in the plane and we chatted on the way. The flight should have been two and three quarter hours but because of fair winds, it was only two hours and fifteen minutes (lucky me). Normally I cannot look out of the plane windows but as we were coming over the coastline and islands of Estonia, I just had to look. My first impression was of lots and lots of pine forests and frozen lakes. I was mesmerised coming to terms with the fact that I was flying over my mother's homeland that it seemed, she would never return to. I immediately burst into tears (of joy I hasten to add). We landed at Tallinn, which was such a lovely small airport, but with obvious building work going on, so I could only hope that it would not be spoiled.

We had to stand behind a yellow line, walk forward one at a time to the booth that had an officer in and when our credentials had been checked, a door was unlocked automatically and so we went through one at a time! Very different to any other airport that I have been through. Ron and I met on the other side of the doors and went to collect

## Estonia and Equines

our baggage. We did not have to wait very long and soon we were through Departures and out to a line of mostly yellow taxis. I just picked a taxi and asked them to take us to the Merchants' Hotel, which was right in the heart of Tallinn Old Town. It was an expensive hotel but I wanted to have a holiday as well as see relations: as I did not know what I would find, I thought I might need a little luxury. We arrived at the hotel and it was lovely and I was getting really excited as Dima and Marian were coming to meet us at the hotel at 1pm.

At five to one I was waiting on the steps of the hotel looking up and down the cobbled street for signs of them. The streets are always full of people as Old Town is a very popular tourist destination and a lot of cruise ships come in. All of a sudden I spotted Uncle Dima in the crowd as he came walking down the cobbled street. I will never forget that first sighting. I recognised him straight away from the photographs that he had sent, even though he had a blue cap on, which I can only liken to a yachting cap and came to learn that it was one of his favourites. In one hand, a bottle of champagne and in his other, some pineapple candies, again, which I came to learn, were his favourites.

Well, I flew up the street and threw my arms around his neck. He hardly speaks a word of English, though that didn't matter. Actions speak louder than words. He came up to Ron and shook hands and he said "Room," in his very deep authoritative voice and we went up the three flights to our room. I was glad then that I had booked an executive suite as we had a sofa in it and some arm chairs and a coffee table. I found some glasses and we opened the bottle. A few seconds later there was a knock at the door and I opened it to see my cousin Marian – also looking just like her photograph –

standing there. We embraced warmly and in she came. A lot of photographs were taken, as we quaffed the champagne.

Marian and I sat side by side on the bed as though it was the most natural thing in the world; as though we had known each other for ages. I don't know how we communicated with each other but we did. Marian had just the English that she had learned at school – so that was a long while ago. About an hour later there was a knock at the door and her oldest son Aarne arrived. His English was virtually word perfect and he turned out to be a very good translator. I guess we were together about four hours and Dima, Marian and Aarne left around 5pm. They were all going home by bus, which was about a twenty-minute journey from the hotel to the outskirts of Old Town. Dima was going to meet us next day at the hotel.

Well I could not stop talking about them all night. They were such fabulous people! Ron and I went for a walk around Old Town and I was surprised at the temperature – it was about nine o'clock in the evening and I was in a short-sleeved top. We had two suitcases of clothes for a very cold place, but it was as if the weather had lifted to join my spirits. After our walk we went into an authentic Estonian restaurant (which soon came to be one of our favourite restaurants), for our evening meal. The staff were all dressed in Estonian costume and Estonian accordion music was playing.

We were not too adventurous that night, so had liver paté served with pickled cucumbers (gherkins to the uninitiated, which I have always absolutely adored, and now know why!) Ron had pork and mash for his main, but I had jellied meat. (I remember Mum making 'brawn' as we would call it in England and I loved that too). In Estonia it is served as an appetiser with boiled potatoes and very, very, very, hot mustard, that the waiter always tells you to be very careful of. I have never tasted anything so hot. Woe betide the people who ignore the warning and treat it as our normal English mustard.

Monday dawned and we got up, showered and went down to the restaurant in the cellar of the hotel for our breakfast, most of which was a buffet. It has since been my experience that most restaurants are in the cellars of the still beautiful merchant houses of this old *hansa* city. They have lovely arched and curved thick walls and are quaint with nooks and crannies. We went back up to our room at nine o'clock and had another hour to wait until we were meeting Dima again.

Promptly, on the dot of ten o'clock, the now familiar figure with the blue cap came jauntily down the road. I did not know then that Dima was 79 and had had a quadruple heart transplant about twenty-five years ago. The only sign was that he had to stop for breath on a few occasions. Off we went with Dima striding on ahead and us following in his wake, up the narrow street, which consisted of a lot of steps to the city on top of the hill. Dima had to stop once only to take breath but we were trailing far behind. Also, he was regaling us with the history of the city in a mixture of broken English, German and Estonian and sign language. Ron is very good interpreting his sign language, so somehow or other it all seemed to gel.

When we got to the top of the steps, there was a big one-foot thick wooden door let into the stone wall around the city. Dima explained that this was locked at night as the rich people lived at the top and they locked it to stop the peasants coming through.

On we marched with Dima explaining as best as he

could what every building was. We were getting rather tired, as this kind of sight-seeing was not the usual holiday for us. We normally relax in the sunshine by a pool but then this was no normal holiday and we were enjoying every minute of it. Dima then took us to the Alexander Nevsky Cathedral. I know that it was built by the Russians, but Dima seemed very proud to show it to us. It is indeed a beautiful place, absolutely dripping in gold and full of tourists looking around. Of course taking photographs is forbidden inside, which is a great pity, as I wanted to show folks back home what an amazing place it is. After walking around for four hours, we were exhausted but Dima looked like he could go on forever talking about his beloved Estonia. His tour was much better than any official guided tour, even if there was a language barrier, but somehow, we all seemed to understand one another.

We were then guided toward a taxi rank and told that we were going back to Dima's flat in Mustamäe. Dima took pity on us as he always travels by trolley bus, but I don't think we had the energy to walk to the bus station. The flats are nothing like ours. Built in the Soviet era in the late Sixties, there were blocks upon blocks of them. Our address was 120-199, which equates to flat number 120 in block 199 so that gives you an idea of how many blocks there were. It was very austere. Unless you have a key to get in you have to buzz to be let in through a plate steel door. Well, in we went. Dima went in the lift, but Ron and I wanted to see the place properly, so despite our tired legs, we walked up the stairs. It is very difficult to describe how forbidding the place seemed with two steel doors opposite one another on each landing and nothing more. We got to 120 and Dima met us by the lift and opened yet another steel door. Once inside there was a steel door to the right, which belonged to Dima's neighbour, and Marian who was waiting for us, opened the steel door on the left to Dima's flat.

In we went. Although the flat looked small from the outside, inside it was quite roomy, containing a hall, a very small kitchen, a toilet and a shower. Halfway down the hall was a room, which was my aunt's bedroom. A bit further on was a living room with a balcony in the front and another room leading from it. Alas, I was not about to meet my aunt Marat as her health had been quite bad and she was still in hospital, but she was coming out on Tuesday so I would get to see her on Wednesday. This day we also met Marian's husband Jaak, and her younger son Erik. Both Erik and Jaak were very shy.

There was plenty to eat: caviar, eggs, soused herrings, salmon, jellied meat (made by Dima), boiled potatoes together with the very very, *very* hot mustard, pickled cucumbers (made by Dima), pickled mushrooms (made by Dima), paté, apple coleslaw (made by Dima) and a good variety of other things that I can't remember. Dima was obviously a very good cook. We found out the dishes were made by Dima because when he had some, he would point to it and say, "My work". Then the vodka started flowing. What I didn't realise was that it is drunk neat in Estonia, with a glass of orange or cranberry juice or something similar by the side. Oh well, when in Rome… (or Estonia in this case!)

There was also champagne again, but that was mainly because it was the only drink that Maret really liked. After the feast came several different types of cake. The meal lasted about four hours during which time Dima came out with a multitude of photographs going back to the early 1900s. He was a stickler for history, which was very lucky for me as it was amazing to look at all the old photographs of my relations. He gave me some lovely ones of my grandfather and one with my mother taken in 1927, so she was only three. The photo that I treasure is of my grandfather show jumping – a photo I never dreamt I would see. I also found out that he had won a big show jumping competition in Hungary. Ron and I had our photograph taken with my aunt Marian, and I thought that we coped with all the vodka very well.

By the end of the day Jaak who had been very shy in the beginning (as Estonians apparently are, and in his case probably because he could not speak a word of English) was sitting next to Ron (who is not shy and who obviously could not speak a word of Estonian) laughing and sharing jokes deep in some sort of conversation, which amused us all as they seemed to be understanding one another with no common language other than signing! Marian took us back to our hotel at around 6pm. What a fantastic day! Better than I could have ever have imagined and what fantastic people my relations really were.

We went for a walk around the Old Town in the balmy May weather in the evening and found a Chinese restaurant, though neither of us was particularly hungry. We picked at some food before wending our way back to the Hotel and falling asleep very quickly.

I was really looking forward to the next day. Once I had found out that I had relations living in Estonia my dream was to ride through the forests just like my grandfather would have done all those years ago. I had spent hours poring over the Internet trying to find riding stables in the country so that I could fulfil my dream. It was quite difficult as it was not yet the start of summer. The horses in Estonia are used for riding in the summer and in the winter they are used for pulling sledges and sleighs. I eventually found one in Aegviidu and communicating by email, made arrangements to go riding on the Tuesday and the Wednesday. The only downside was that the stables were sixty miles away. Luckily they did a collection service by car and so at 9 o'clock in the morning the car arrived to collect us. It had a fabulous picture on the side, which, I assumed, was something to do with the stables, and was similar to the picture on the website.

Our driver, who was also the owner of the stables, was called Ülla Rink. She was very nice and could speak very good English so the sixty-mile journey passed very quickly. Also, on the way, she pointed out all the buildings that were of historical interest. Below is the advertisement that I found on the web.

---

```
Kivisaare farm in Aegviidu about 70
km from Tallinn offers accommodation
(breakfast, sauna, rooms with
fireplace) and facilities for riding
in the forest. A beautiful lake for
swimming is on 150 m. In winter
time we arrange skiing tracks
for cross-country skiing.NAME:
Kivisaare ratsataluADDRESS: Järve
tn. 10 Aegviidu, 74501 Harjumaa,
EstoniaGPS: 25°37'55'' E, 59°16'31''
NGSM: (372) 5663 1520Fax: (372) 657
5436E-mail: **kivisaare@maaturism.ee**
Skype: KivisaareLANDLADY Ülle Rink
Welcome: do ride to Aegviidu!
```

# FIRST VISIT

Aegviidu is the heart of Kõrvemaa. Its face was carved during the glacial epoch by the playful forces of nature. Here are hills covered with forests, beautiful little lakes, hillocks and ridges, shady paths and small streams purling in the meadows. Noble pines and firs stretch out to the sky. Forests full of bilberries and wooded heathers alternate with bogs and marshy lands. Seven lakes on which ancient trees reflect, give Aegviidu a special magical feeling. Dim evenings bring fog over the lakes and lonely fish splash in the water. It is very quiet.The district of Aegviidu is in the middle of Kõrvemaa, where Tapa — Tallinn railway and Piibe highway meet. Aegviidu district with its population of little more than one thousand inhabitants is the smallest district in Harjumaa. Aegviidu got its rights as a county town in 1945. Historically it has belonged to Järvamaa Lehtse district, but since 1962 it was given to Harjumaa.Aegviidu was first mentioned in 1796 on the Mellini map of Livonia and was called back then Aegwid. The name

```
itself does not come from the
words "to have a good time" but
is supposedly originated from the
18th century when Piibe highway
was built through swamps and bogs.
The construction works took a long
time and thus the name Aegviidu was
born.Come enjoy riding! We offer you
and your family an opportunity to
spend several hours, the entire day
or even the entire weekend riding
in open air. Here in Aegviidu you
can learn to ride, take short trips
into a beautiful forest or take
part in all day lasting expedition
to Kõrvemaa.All the riding will be
supervised by experienced trainers.
```

Ron and I expected to see stables similar to those in England, but the only building was the house, and a field which had a couple of tyres and poles in, and a log store.

We got out and were given a tour of the house. It is used as a farmhouse for staying in and has saunas etc. It was very nice but not what we had gone there for. There seemed to be only one other person there who was a young girl helper (who I later found out Ülle had previously collected in Tallinn). There were three horses in the middle of the field, which were caught and tied up to a fence pole each. I was told that I had the choice of Karamella, which a palomino horse, about 15.3hh, a 4-year-old bay that had just been broken in and about 15hh and a grey pony that was about 14hh at a push.

## FIRST VISIT

Well, I decided that I had better go for the biggest one and so chose Karamella, and then proceeded to brush her down. She was very good and we proceeded to get on like a house on fire. Ülle did tell me that the only thing that she did not like was big dogs and she could rear up and try to turn and flee. Oh well, I decided, I would have to take my chance. The tack was retrieved from the log store and they gave the saddle and bridle to fit Karamella and I tacked her up. Ülle decided that she would ride the 4-year-old and that left the grey pony for the helper.

I always use a mounting block at home – it is easier for the horse instead of pulling the saddle over as you mount from the ground – but alas no such thing existed there. So we improvised. I had a little hop up and then a chair and then another wobbly box, and with the Ron holding all so that it did not tip over, I somehow managed to climb aboard!

I was still waiting for Ülle and the helper to tack-up their steeds and had to sit there for about half an hour. At last they were ready. All three of us were aboard and then Ülle realised that she did not have her hat so dismounted, ran back indoors and came out with her hat. Once more we were all aboard and then Ülle realised that she had the wrong footwear on and once again dismounted and went into the house. Five minutes later she came out minus trainers and equipped with proper riding boots. Hoorah! At last we were underway. Whilst I had been sitting there patiently waiting, Ron was armed with the camera to take lots of photos of me doing the thing that I never ever dreamt would happen: in the country, on horseback in Estonia. Ron snapped me on Karamella and then we were underway.

We rode round the field and made for the main road. Just before the end of the road there were a couple of rural houses with sheds, chickens etc. and, oh my, what did I see? Great big dogs running around and barking. The fence around the property was only a see-through wire fence, so I thought to myself, "Well, here comes test number one".

I could feel Karamella getting tense and, as we approached, I waited for the rear and bolt back towards home. I asked her to walk on, put my hand on her neck and told her mentally all was well and all she did, bless her, was about three steps of 'trot' and walked right on past. I considered that Karamella and myself had passed the first test with flying colours. We continued to the main road, crossed, (I was pleased to say that we were all wearing yellow reflective jackets, which is apparently the law in Estonia – I wish it was in this country!) and within twenty yards were ensconced in a beautiful pine forest. Ron said he would come behind us and take photos as we were walking along. We went a little way down the track and then veered off left up the hill into the trees. I suppose that there was a track there but I could not see it and just followed Ülle, who was in front on the youngster.

Karamella was absolutely amazing. She wended her way over tree roots that no English riding horse could have done, in such a sure-footed way. I was a bit apprehensive to start with, but needn't have worried and after ten minutes of 'wending' was feeling quite confident. Then we approached a tree that had blown down in the middle of all the undergrowth. Well, in England, it would have been the sort of thing that would have been lovely to 'pop' over and so I wondered how we were going to negotiate this obstacle as there it was surrounded by undergrowth. Karamella did not 'bat at an eyelid'. She just walked up to it and lifted one front leg over, then the other and then her hind legs in the same manner – very smoothly. It just goes to show how different horses adapt to different riding country.

We emerged from the 'non-track' onto another track at the top of a hill (this had obviously been a short-cut that the horses were used to). We walked down one side and then I was told we were going to gallop up the other steep side. Being used to riding a 16.3hh thoroughbred racehorse at home, it was very different riding Karamella (a 15.3hh very wide, heavy horse), but we charged up the hill and it was very weird – like riding a rocking-horse. Unfortunately, when I pulled her up, I felt that she was very slightly unsound in front. I told Ülle, and she said that if I wanted we could go back to the stables and she would get me another horse to ride (I have no idea where from). As we had been out for some time and the mare was sound at a walk, I decided that I was quite happy walking around the forest and did not have to go galloping everywhere. The mare might just have bruised her frog on a tree root and I thought that we were about half way through our ride anyway.

We continued traversing through the forest, which was really unique: very quiet and peaceful. I learned that the route we had taken was known as the 'Five Lakes' ride: Viis Jarva. All of a sudden we came to a clearing with a lovely house by a lake. What a setting. Ülle informed me that in the summer when the rides came this way, all the horses had halters on under their bridles. Everyone would dismount, tie their steed to the appropriate tree or bush and go swimming for an hour. Just as well it wasn't summer as there were no visible mounting places and so I would not have been able to get on again. Anyway we just sat there a while and took in the scenery, which was stunning.

## Estonia and Equines

After a little while we moved off again and now we were really deep into the woods. We kept coming to crossways, which had wooden signposts pointing in every direction. Ülle explained that they were used more in the winter as the paths for the skiers. I had totally lost my sense of direction by now, but was loving every minute of it. We came to a wooden bridge with no sides across a river and had to cross it. Ülle's youngster was not very keen and though she made several attempts to get her horse over the bridge, she refused to go. This is where the little grey pony came into its own and just walked across followed by Ülle on the youngster and then me on Karamella. The paths through the forest were in straight lines and I discovered that hundreds of years ago they were the paths that were used by merchants.

I forgot to mention that while we were on our way down to Aegviidu in the car with Ülle, she did mention that brown bears lived in the woods and you had to be careful when driving, especially in the winter as they would just appear and dash across the road. I never really found out how big they were but I was praying that we did not run into one on our ride! As luck would have it we did not see anything untoward!

We traversed a lot more *hansa* (merchant) paths and then came out into a clearing with a little wooden house and an old man who looked about 100-years-old, but was probably only 70-ish. Ülle stopped and spoke to him and I tried out my poor Estonian. "Tere hommikust," I said: "Good morning." He gave me a lovely smile and said "Tere hommikust." We passed by his house and then all of a sudden we were back in civilisation, about a hundred yards up the main road that we had crossed about two hours earlier. I un-tacked Karamella and left our helper to deal with the horses, although I don't know what happened as there were no stables to put them into! Ron and I got into Ülle's car and started the sixty-mile journey back to our hotel in Tallinn.

Unfortunately, because I had been sat on Karamella for about an hour before we got underway, and also because she was so wide and a completely different shape to Charlie, my Thoroughbred, my hip had really started aching. I didn't really care as I'd had such a wonderful time. I had booked to go riding for two days and so Ülle was going to collect me again in the morning. I didn't think that my hip would stick another ride, even though Ülle did say that she would get another horse for me from a friend. I decided when we got back to our hotel that my hip had had enough. I had done what I wanted to do, and so I paid Ülle for the day that I was not having (so I don't think that she minded too much) and Ron and I went to our room, showered and changed and went out to our favourite Estonian restaurant for lunch, followed by a relaxing afternoon and back to the same place for our evening meal. The only downside to the day was that Ron told me that after he took the one picture of me on Karamella, it was the last picture and the film had wound on to the end, so I had no photographs of my riding through that wonderful pine forest.

The next day was a most relaxing day. We walked round the outskirts of old town and in the main square was a market so we spent a lovely time looking at all the stalls. The weather was absolutely beautiful and we sat outside 'Karl Freidrich' in the square, on decking in the glorious sunshine and had a couple of drinks and our lunch. It was very hot and I burnt my arms and a bright red V around my neck! We went back to the hotel and had a snooze and watched TV. We were looking forward to the evening as I had booked a special package, which included a meal in the restaurant on a night of our choice, and tonight was the night. Much later, after a lovely meal and a memorable evening, I tumbled into bed a very happy person after four wonderful days in Estonia.

The following day we planned to meet Marian and Dima in the morning. We were up early and went down to the end of Old Town to a fantastic street that had little flower shops all down one side. I bought some lovely flowers, one bouquet for Marian and one for my aunt Maret, who was out of hospital and I was going to be able to meet later in the day for the first time.

Marian and Dima arrived about 11am. I gave Marian her bouquet and we linked arms and walked on through Old Town, out to the car park on the edge of the new town, which is where Marian had parked her car after collecting her father, Dima. My aunt, I was told, was too unwell to come with us, and was at home in her bedroom, but she was well enough to be left for a couple of hours. So, off we went again. Marian took us around the beautiful park and showed us the Parliament House. We seemed to drive for a bit and then park and walk for a bit. Both Marian and my uncle were so proud of their country and wanted to show us everything that they could.

Kadriorg can be considered to be the grandest example of a palace and park design in Estonian architectural history. The palace, originally an Imperial summer residence, has been extremely well preserved since the early eighteenth century. Designed to resemble the Italian palaces of the time, the palace has a façade which has three levels at the front and sides and two levels at the rear in a mix of architectural styles. A banquet hall and winter garden were added to the rear facade of the palace in 1933/34.

FIRST VISIT

We then went on the road to Pringi, which is where Dima has a country cottage. They wanted to show it to us and also make sure that everything was okay there. Dima and Maret live there from around 1st May to 1st October. Of course it is dependent on the weather, but that was the usual time. Because aunt Maret had not been well they had not moved out there yet. It was lovely. We drove along the coast road and then the house was about a hundred yards inland from the sea. We parked, got out and were shown all round it. It seemed very Scandinavian. On the wall in the living room was a framed photo that I had sent to them of our wedding. It was in black and white (well, we did get married in 1970, and only black and white photos were available in those days, though it would probably be considered chic now!) and showed, as well as me and Ron, Astrid, (my Mum), my Dad, and Ron's Mum and Dad. The cottage is very secluded and has a lovely garden where Dima likes nothing more that to have the neighbours round in the summer for a barbecue of smoked fish, and of course the requisite vodka.

After our tour, we drove the hundred yards to the main road and then parked again outside what looked like a great big upturned wooden boat. There was a small outdoor museum next to it which we looked round. We were right by the sea and there were tiny thatched huts that the people used to live in with their animals many years ago. It was quite cold and we took more photographs and then went back to the upturned boat which turned out to be a restaurant! Of course in we went for another meal. We all had fish, which was great, and soon we were back in the car heading back to Tallinn.

Uncle Dima had other ideas and called for another stop by a big statue of an angel pointing out to sea. He told us through Marian that an Estonian ship had gone down

## Estonia and Equines

there whilst trying to defend the country and the angel was pointing to the men. This was the Russalka Memorial, a bronze monument sculpted by Amandus Adamson, erected on 7 September 1902 in Kadriorg, Tallinn, to mark the ninth anniversary of the sinking of the Russian warship Russalka, or 'Mermaid,' which sank en route to Finland in 1893. The monument depicts an angel holding an Orthodox cross towards the assumed direction of the shipwreck. During the Soviet rule the cross was removed and the angel pointed to the sea with her bare hand. The model for the angel was the sculptor's housekeeper, Juliana Rootsi, whose grandson is the politician Tiit Made.

Finally we were back in the car and on our way back to Dima's flat in Mustamäe. At last I was to meet my aunt Maret, Mum's sister. When we arrived back at the flat, Marian went to see her mother. It seemed that her health had really deteriorated a lot more that her sister's. Her body was worse but funnily enough her mind was better than my Mum's. I went in to see her, bent over and kissed her, as she was laying on a single bed and she knew who I was. She couldn't speak any English, so I said the few words of Estonian that I had learnt. "Tere tadi Maret, kuidas sa elad?" (Hello, aunt Maret, how are you?) With that I went back to the living room where another great feast had been prepared and spread out on the table. Maret got up and came and sat in her chair in the living room, but before she sat down, she came over to me with a necklace of Estonian amber and gave it to me, which was a lovely thought and confirmed to me that she knew who I was.

We spent another evening eating and drinking and then Marian took us back to the hotel. We were to have the following day to ourselves and then were meeting up in Old Town as Ron and I wanted to take them all out for meal to whichever restaurant they chose. Dima used to go to Azerbaijan a lot and loved their hot food and so luckily, we found an Azerbaijani restaurant in Tallinn Old Town. We all met outside our hotel and walked to the restaurant, where we had a memorable meal. Jaak had to go to work so he left from the restaurant, but Marian, Dima and Aarne insisted on walking us back to our hotel, where we said our goodbyes as we were flying home the next day. Surprisingly, I ended up in tears when Marian asked, "Will you come back again?" I said, "Of course," and really hoped so. We sadly parted, as our six-day whirlwind visit to Estonia had almost come to an end.

The next day we bade our sad farewell of Tallinn and started the long journey home. Tallinn to Stanstad. Stansted to Newquay, then a taxi to pick us up at the airport. Our suitcases were so full of 'goodies' from Dima that although it was okay for Easyjet, we had to pay £84 for extra weight on the Ryanair trip back to Newquay. To cap it all, the pilot 'missed the runway' at Newquay and we had to go round again to land. It was a beautiful flying day, so I hadn't been too worried about the flight, but I was when we suddenly whooshed up in the air again. Our taxi driver wondered what had happened when he saw the plane take off again and so did we! When we finally landed and got off there were fire trucks and men with 'Emergency' on the backs of their uniforms everywhere. I never did find out the reason why the pilot missed the landing strip and somehow or other all this did not put me off flying, and I started planning our next trip to Estonia the following year.

I couldn't wait to tell Mum where I had been, and that I had met her sister, and show her the photographs that I had brought back with me. Unfortunately, although she knew that she was Estonian and that Tallinn was the capital, that was about it. She did not recognise anyone from the photos. I had even slipped in a photo of Ron but she did not recognise him either, even though he was sitting next to her. It was all very, very sad.

# OUR SECOND VISIT TO ESTONIA IN 2009

I arranged our next trip for Easter in 2009. There was no way that I was flying with Ryanair again so we had a taxi from Devon to Stansted. What a drive! We stayed in a lovely pub on 4th April – The Swan in Dunmow, although that nearly ended in disaster. We arrived at lunchtime and, including the taxi driver, had a meal. I thought I had better mention that we were staying there when I got another drink. I had booked our room online through Late Rooms, but it turned out that they had not got the booking. The landlord asked me if I was in the right place because there was another Swan very close by. Well, I went and got my print out to prove it, but I knew that I was in the right place as I had a picture of it. Oh dear, we were in the right place – but they weren't expecting us! The landlord got on the phone to his wife straight away and told her to get over to the pub as soon as she could, as he had a booking and we were there and the room needed making up. Ron went to get the suitcases from the taxi and I waited outside at the bottom of the stairs to the rooms. All of a sudden this puffed-out lady appeared and said that she had been called over by some guests that had suddenly arrived, and who were very irate but weren't even here, and there she was, rushing specially to see us in. I just looked at her and pointed to myself. Oh dear – she didn't know what to do or say! The upshot being that we had a very nice evening and stay, and nothing was too much trouble! And so on Saturday 5th April we were once more on our way to Estonia.

Our trip in 2009 was very similar to 2008, except for the weather, because we were a month earlier. As we flew in over Tallinn we could see that everything was frozen: all the lakes (of which there are many), and even the shoreline of the sea. We were also staying at a different hotel, St Petersburg. It was about twenty yards further up the side street from our last hotel, but whereas Merchants' House had been an Estonian Hotel, St Petersburg belonged to a Russian chain of hotels. Merchants' House had been a modern hotel in an old building with a nice trendy bar, but St Petersburg was the opulent Russia of years ago. The staff uniforms were wonderful, and even the cleaners looked like guests. There was a big wide sweeping staircase leading to the first floor, where our room was situated, which was beautifully carpeted.

The bar doubled as the breakfast room in the morning and it was lovely with fantastic oil paintings of rich people and Tsars from years ago. Breakfasts were cooked to order and beautifully served. In the evening there was Russian music in the bar: a violinist and a female accordionist who also sang, playing Russian songs like 'Kalinka' and the violinist played 'Czardas' (which I know is a Hungarian piece but it sounds Russian to me).

Marian had a few days of holiday away from work (she is the manager of a big kitchen that makes about one thousand different lines for a chain of supermarkets called Selver. They are in Estonia, Latvia and Lithuania. The kitchen makes many varieties of salads, desserts and cakes). Marian and her best friend from her childhood days, Katrin, both work in the same office at Selver. Katrin searches out suppliers. We met Marian on the outskirts of Old Town and we were off on a whirlwind tour again. The day was fairly pleasant and we went to the stadium where the Singing Revolution was held. It had such atmosphere. We sat in the grounds and had a picnic.

The Singing Revolution is a commonly used name for events between 1987 and 1991 that led to the restoration of the independence of Estonia, Latvia and Lithuania. The term was coined by an Estonian activist and artist called Heinz Valk, from an article about spontaneous mass night-singing demonstrations, at the Tallinn Song Festival Grounds.

On 11 September 1988, a massive song festival, called 'Song of Estonia' was held at the Tallinn Song Festival Arena. This time nearly 300,000 people came together, more than a quarter of all Estonians. On that day political leaders were participating actively, and were for the first time insisting on the restoration of independence.

On 16 November 1988, the legislative body of Estonia issued the Estonian Sovereignty Declaration. In 1990 Estonia had been the first Soviet republic to defy the Soviet army by offering alternative service to Estonian residents scheduled to be drafted. Most Estonians, however, simply began avoiding the draft.

The Singing Revolution lasted over four years, with various protests and acts of defiance. In 1991, as Soviet tanks attempted to stop the progress towards independence, the Estonian Supreme Soviet together with the Congress of

## Estonia and Equines

Estonia proclaimed the restoration of the independent state of Estonia and repudiated Soviet legislation. People acted as human shields to protect radio and TV stations from the Soviet tanks. Through these actions Estonia regained its independence without any bloodshed.

On 22 August 1991, Iceland became the first nation to recognise the newly restored independence of Estonia. Today, a plaque commemorating this event is situated on the outside wall of the Foreign Ministry, which itself is situated on Islandi Väljak 1, or Iceland Square 1. The plaque reads; "The Republic of Iceland was the first to recognize, on 22 August 1991, the restoration of the independence of the Republic of Estonia", in Estonian, Icelandic and English.

Independence was declared on the late evening of August 20, 1991, after an agreement between different political parties was reached. The next morning Soviet troops, according to Estonian TV, attempted to storm Tallinn TV Tower but were not successful. The Communist hardliners' coup attempt failed amid mass pro-democracy demonstrations in Moscow led by Boris Yeltsin.

I was learning so much about my mother's homeland.

After that we went back to Dima's flat for, yes you've guessed it, another big spread.

The next day we had a day of rest and then on Wednesday we met Dima and Marian and they took us to a restored mill that served great food. I was told we were going to eat salmon, but in reality it was a fish like our rainbow trout. When we arrived what I hadn't been told was that we would all be given a rod and would have to catch the fish ourselves! That turned out to be a bit of a joke and there was the option to let the owner of the restaurant do it for you. As I do not like to see anything living if I am going to eat it (I think I could easily become a vegetarian), I quickly dashed inside and left everyone else outside laughing at me.

Well, our Maître d' caught the fish and we did, indeed, have a delicious meal and then back to our hotel.

# RAKVERE

As I mentioned, Marian is in charge of the kitchens in Tallinn that make all the salads, desserts etc. to sell in the Selver chain of supermarkets. There are thirty-four of them, in all, in Estonia and more, I think, in Latvia. Marian arranged for us to go and see the Selver in Rakvere, the place where I believe my mother was living when her father was arrested in 1941. Off we set in Hugo, the little works van. Marian and her best friend Katrin were in the front, and Ron and myself in the back. It was surprisingly comfortable. The weather was awful though – dull and raining hard. Marian stayed with us as it was Katrin who was doing the inspecting at this store. Whilst Katrin was busy, Marian took us to the fort on the hill. In the summer it is opened as a museum but she had rung and apparently they'd had a party of tourists booked in and so agreed to let us have a look around too. What a beautiful view from the top.

After we looked around the museum, we went into the actual fort and the curator who was dressed as a monk showed us inside. There were the usual touristy gimmicks; we went into one room that had a torture chamber and a tomb in, and all of a sudden the lights dimmed and there was an awful noise and a skeleton covered in cobwebs arose from the tomb and frightened me to death! That was enough for me. The monk then took us down into the depths and we were going to be led through some catacombs – but not me, I'm afraid! I suddenly turned into a wimp of the highest order as I could imagine what was going to happen. They tried to persuade me but I wouldn't give way, so the monk said I could stay outside and wait. Ron and Marian disappeared inside and I saw the monk with his robes flowing behind him vanish into a side room. I heard awful banging and crashing and wailing and then organ music. Then I heard Marian shrieking and then laughing.

I was so glad that I had refrained from going in. Marian and Ron appeared in fits of laughter. Apparently they had to nearly crouch down to get along and then the floor started shaking and the monk jumped out in front of them. What a 'wuss' I was. Never mind. Ron and Marian enjoyed it. We then met up with Katrin and went for a meal before the hundred-kilometre drive back to Tallinn.

Rakvere is also known now for its 'Tarvas' – statue of an auroch (an ancient, massive cow), which was made by the Estonian sculptor Tauno Kangro. It is thought to be the largest animal statue in the Baltic countries. It is situated on the edge of Vallimägi hill and was erected for the town's 700th birthday. Along with the granite block it sits on, the statue is seven meters long, four meters high and weighs about seven tons. The statue is made out of bronze. The names of the companies and private people who financed it are engraved in the granite block.

Well, as it inevitably does, our last day arrived, which was a Saturday, and as she was not at work, we were going to

Marian's for lunch. We got a taxi to her place, which was a similar flat to Dima's, in a similar type of building. Jaak did the cooking and what a cook he is. We had fantastic roast pork, with roast potatoes. There was fried cabbage as well, which Ron loves, but that is one thing that I do not like. Katrin, Marian's friend called in and she had made a lovely cheesecake for us all. Well, the vodka was flowing again, and so we spent several happy hours eating and drinking. I think that it was about 9 o'clock when we decided to leave. I thought that Ron was looking a bit worse for wear but he pulled himself together and traversed the four flights of stairs quite well so I thought that he was okay.

Marian took us back to our drop off point, just on the edge of Old Town. Out we got and said our goodbyes and waved Marian off back to Mustamäe, and then Ron said his legs did not feel too good. I thought he was messing around, but apparently not, because as he put it, a drainpipe jumped out in front of him and he went down onto his knees. The 'Saaremaa' had something to answer for! I had heck of a job, but managed to get him upright and helped him to the hotel. I said to him, "You get up those stairs while I get the key from reception". When I turned around he was head down, watching his feet, willing them on, marching up and around the sweep of the staircase. I arrived at the top of the stairs and he had managed to find the correct room and was leaning on the wall outside the door. It was still quite early in the evening and we had decided that we were going out for a Chinese meal for some obscure reason. Well, that was the end of that!

Ron went straight to bed and was snoring within ten seconds. Boy was I mad! I was looking forward to my Chinese! I raided the fridge for some food and picked out what I thought were peanuts, opened the packet, shovelled some in my mouth and crunch. What I thought were peanuts were in fact shell-on pistachios. Ouch! That made me even more mad!

The next morning, Ron was bright as a button and I had a chipped tooth! After breakfast we set off to the airport for our long trip back to Devon, already looking forward to our trip back the following year.

# SAD NEWS AND THIRD (UNINTENTIONAL) VISIT

As always in life, nothing ever goes as you plan it. On Wednesday 9th September 2009, I received this devastating piece of news, which of course, really upset me. One minute I had found my aunt and the next minute she had been taken away from me. I was just so glad that I had been able to meet with her and that she had known who I was.

---

```
Dear Ann and Ron

I have to inform you that
yesterday, around 2 o'clock, my
mother, Maret passed away. Dima
gave her lunch and after she ate
it, she became quiet. The ambulance
```

## SAD NEWS AND THIRD (UNINTENTIONAL) VISIT

came in five minutes, but there was nothing they could do — they only noted the death. Dima is very sad and broken, but we support him. Dima decided to stay at the summer cottage because there are things to do there. He will be returningin the end of October. Today I had a free day from work to get Maret's paperwork in order and arrange the funeral. The funeral is held on Saturday. Light a candle and keep her in mind.

I will send you the pictures from the funeral later.

With Love Marian

---

Dear Marian

I was so upset to receive your letter; it certainly was a great shock. My computer is not working at home and so I received it on Thursday morning at work. I hope that you and Dima are coping - Ron and I were really worried about Dima. I tried to see if I could book a flight on Friday so that we could be at the funeral but there was no way that we could get to the airport by 7.30 on the Friday morning. Our thoughts were with you all day on Saturday. We lit a candle for Maret and I hope that the flowers arrived in time.

I will write later.

Our love to you all.

Love

Ann and Ron xx

---

Dear Ann

Thank you for the flowers, which arrived at time. We took them to the funeral and placed them later on the grave. The funeral ceremony was modest but nice. There where about thirty-five people. For Aarne and Erik it was very hard and sad, because it was their first funeral. Dima pulled through surprisingly well. Maret was cremated. I'll get the urn with the ashes next week and then we have to find time to

bury it in the cemetery. We will
bury the ashes in the same place
where Dima's parents are buried.
I also made pictures from the
funeral, but haven't yet developed
them. We try to move on with our
lives step by step. I'm still very
busy at work. I just came back
from Latvia. Dima is working in
our summer cottage and he is doing
better.

Love

Marian

---

Hi Ann and Ron

I informed Dima that you will be
coming soon. At the moment I don't
know, is Dima at the summer cottage
or not. Today he went there and
wants to stay for a week, depends
on the weather. But recently he
was ill for 3 days, as usual in
September. Wherever Dima is, we
will be still waiting for your
arrival. Please write me exactly
when you come and how long you will
be staying, like I said I have

few holiday days. So I can manage them, because I can't get the all week off from work. Time flies, today is a month past from my mother's departure. When you come, we will go and bury the ashes.

See you soon

Marian

---

Dear Marian

We are sorry to hear that Dima has been unwell and hope that he will soon recover. I have booked the flight and we leave on Saturday 24th October. It is at 6.45 am in the morning so it will be a very long Friday night as it is a six hour drive to the airport so we shall have to drive through the night to arrive at 4.45 am to check in. We shall be tired when we arrive. I will book a hotel in Tallinn and we can always get a taxi from there. We shall return on Saturday 31st October but that is nice as we arrive in England at 14.25 so will drive back home

## SAD NEWS AND THIRD (UNINTENTIONAL) VISIT

mostly in the daylight.

I cannot believe that it is a month since Maret passed away - you are right time flies. I also did not think that we would be back to Estonia this year!

Thank you for waiting to bury the ashes - we will be upset but at least we will be there.

I will let you know which hotel I have managed to book. Hopefully Ron will have his teeth - scheduled for next Wednesday!

Love to all

Ann

---

Dear Marian

I have been told at work today that my hours have been cut and so I have to lose 33% of my wages! Still at the moment at least I have a job! I have booked a hotel and it is St Olav in Old Town. Ron got his teeth yesterday, but they are

```
really loose and keep falling out
of his mouth!

He ate a sandwich and they got
stuck in them. He has to go back
to the dentist on Friday again to
see what they can do about it! I
hope it is sorted before we come
to Estonia. I will ring you when
we get to our room in St Olav. We
cannot check in until after 2pm.

I hope that Dima is fully recovered
now and we are really looking
forward to seeing you all again.

Love

Ann
```

And so it was that we were returning to Estonia under not very happy circumstances, a lot sooner that I had thought!

It was nice to see Marian, Dima, Jaak, Aaren and Erik again but it was also very sad. And so it was that we buried aunt Maret's ashes on 27th October in Pärnamäe cemetery on the way to Maardu Village. Established in 1963, Pärnamäe Cemetery quickly grew into the nation's largest place of final rest. Though it doesn't have nearly as many VIPs as Metsakalmistu, it nevertheless has dozens of monuments and artistically-designed grave sites.

It was a really beautiful place, if a cemetery can be

called that. All the graves are beautifully looked after. We had been to buy some flowers in the morning and I also bought a rose that we could plant. We were there for about an hour. We planted our flowers, lit candles, and said our private prayers. I thought that I would be okay but, of course, I burst into tears and then that upset Marian.

# APELSIN

Marian told us that she would meet us again the next day at our hotel and that she had bought tickets to see Apelsin (which is the Estonian word for orange, who had a been a rock/country group from years ago and were having a 25 year celebration at the Suur Halle, the biggest theatre in Tallinn). We went along with open minds thinking that we probably would not enjoy it as much as we should, as we could not speak the language. Well, it was a fantastic evening and they sang a lot of songs that we knew like 'Green Green Grass of Home' and 'She Taught Me How to Yodel' that had been sung by Frank Ifield. They were great musicians and played and sang for two and a half hours nonstop. It certainly cheered us all up.

It was on the way back to the hotel that I had one of the creepiest experiences of my life. Marian had said goodbye to us outside the concert hall, and as she did so, realised that she had left one of her leather gloves in the foyer. She came back, found us and we all went back to the concert hall, and there it was still on the seat where she had left it. Amazing. We said goodbye again and started walking back from the new town to our hotel in the Old Town. I hadn't noticed but Ron said later that he had noticed a man and a woman (English, by the way) walking very close behind us, talking. Anyway, we had walked across the town square, which was fairly busy, and had got to about fifty yards from our hotel (actually, outside our favourite restaurant, as we were going for a late meal, which meant we were walking up a cobbled side street).

The pavement was only wide enough to walk single file, and so Ron had moved on in front of me, though we were still carrying on a conversation, and I was dawdling a bit. The couple behind me drew alongside and I took no notice as I was talking to Ron. I had my handbag on my shoulder and all of a sudden I felt the flap which was obviously on the outside being slowly lifted. It still didn't dawn on me what was happening and so I just clamped my arm down on my bag and walked faster to catch Ron up, and the two people behind me dived into a doorway on my right, and disappeared.

My brain was still mulling it over when in another couple of yards we had reached our restaurant, went in and sat down. All of a sudden I realised what they were doing. Pick-pocketing! Or pick-handbagging in my case! They would have been out of luck anyway even if they had managed to do it without my realising what was going on, because the only thing in my handbag was my makeup bag, containing nothing of value! Ron kept all the money and credit cards inside the pocket of his shirt underneath his jacket. I mulled it over in my mind deciding whether to tell Ron or not. Eventually, I decided to and he said that he thought it was peculiar as he had noticed them following us since we entered the gates of Old Town which was about a thousand yards from where they attempted to pick-handbag me. He thought it was funny because they were walking very close behind but did not overtake us. When they aborted their mission and disappeared he said he had wondered where they had gone and I told him that they had disappeared very quickly into the Havana Cigar Smoking Emporium.

The more I thought about it the more it brought a shiver to my spine – it was the horrible feeling of the flap of my handbag slowly being lifted. They'd have to do a bit more practise to make perfect, but I hope they never do! It was a great shame as it spoiled an otherwise fantastic evening.

I told Marian the next day and she was horrified and from then on I never even took a bag with me in the evenings.

Friday came along, and it was our last night again. Everyone came to meet us outside the hotel and we were going to take them all for a meal, but where to go? Marian decided she would like to try some Greek food and we had seen a Greek restaurant at the top of Old Town, so we all climbed the wretched steps again. We had a very nice meal, although it was not authentic Greek; it was Greek food cooked by non-Greeks, so could never be the real thing, but Marian and family enjoyed it and we all enjoyed the evening. They walked us back down to our hotel and we said our goodbyes again with the promise that we would return the next year.

Sometime after we'd returned home, they sent us a photo, showing us their visit to the summer cottage just after we left, to see if all was well. They spent three hours digging through the snow drifts just to get in and around the cottage. The snow was up to the window ledges. The thing that I find most peculiar is that in Estonia, everything keeps going in the snow and the roads are all clear. Here in the UK, one small flurry of two or three inches of snow and the whole country comes to a standstill – though I certainly do not want to experience twenty-five degrees under. It is always very cold when you go to Estonia in March but I do not feel that cold, and all the houses, coffee shops and restaurants are all beautifully warm inside. My uncle's flat is lovely and warm. I am not sure how it is heated but it looks like a very antiquated system of radiators – but, as the old adage goes, the old ones are the best!

# FOURTH VISIT (INCLUDING SAAREMAA)

Dear Ann and Ron

I understood that you will arrive here Friday night. Get well rested and we will be waiting for you at two o'clock, Dima's place, Saturday. I booked you a stay for few days at a Spa hotel in Saaremaa, the date is 16-17.04. It is a small and comfortable hotel in the middle of Kuresaare city. I will link to you the homepage, if you can open it. www.johan.ee. Bring your swimsuits, if you want to swim in the pool.

FOURTH VISIT (INCLUDING SAAREMAA)

Til we meet in Tallinn.

Marian, Aarne, Erik, Jaak

---

Kallis Marian

Tere

Have just got into work and read your email. Only two more days at work until we begin the long journey. We are both looking forward to our trip and yesterday morning we played Apelsin really loud (to get in the mood Ron said!) I managed to get into the hotel website and it looks great. Would you believe that we had snow again last Wednesday but it has warmed up a bit again since then. The temperatures do not look too bad in Tallinn at the moment. Aarne must be finding it tropical after -20C etc!! We hope that Dima is well.

Looking forward to seeing everyone again.

Kuni kell kaks laupäeval majas Dima ja üks suur TERVISEKS!!!

```
Estonia and Equines

Näeme varsti Tallinnas ja Kõik meie
armastus

Ann ja Ron
```

We decided to stay in the same hotel, the St Olav, that we had used the previous October. It is very close to the Old Town square and we were now friendly with Erik the hotel manager who gave us a good price for the room as we were staying for a fortnight. Forty euros a night, instead of sixty-two as per the Internet, and also an upgrade on the room. Not bad.

The plane was delayed and so we did not land until 23.30, and by the time we got our luggage and got to St Olav it was midnight. We checked in and then rushed off to the Square as we were really hungry. It is amazing that at one o'clock in the morning, the Square was full of people, sitting, eating and drinking outside bars under patio warmer lamps and wrapped in rugs. So Ron and I did the same.

The next day we got a taxi to Mustamäe to Dima's flat and the next few days followed our normal routines.

On the Friday, Marian brought us a weekend bag and we packed our overnight things to get ready for our trip to Saaremaa. Marian had booked this because Saaremaa is my favourite brand of vodka. It is also an island off the coast and so Marian being Marian booked us the trip.

She collected us on Saturday morning and took us to the bus station where she waited with us and put us on the coach like a couple of school children. The coach was very full and she had a word with the coach driver and though I have no idea what she said, I suspect that she asked him to look after us! Ron had not been looking forward to the trip but as

## FOURTH VISIT (INCLUDING SAAREMAA)

it turned out it was brilliant and we both thoroughly enjoyed it.

Saaremaa, which is around, two thousand seven hundred km² and has a population of around thirty-five thousand inhabitants is the largest of Estonia's islands. Although there are various routes the 'easiest' way to get to the island of Saaremaa is via Tallinn.

The journey was scheduled to last for four and a half hours – which I think was why Ron was not looking forward to it as he thought we would be sitting for a long time – but, the coach driver was very good and we had a very smooth journey. The trip from the mainland of Estonia passes through some of the country's most beautiful scenery. In particular the stretch from Muhu on to Saaremaa makes the journey more than worthwhile!

Once negotiating your way out of Tallinn the journey is quite simple. You travel southwest towards Virtsu and take the short (thirty minute) ferry ride to the island of Muhu, which is linked by a bridge to Saaremaa. Estonian roads, once outside Tallinn are very quiet and a joy to drive along. You should look out for the moose (who are not known for their intelligence and tend to wander onto roads) and the other abundant wildlife in Estonia, including bears. Once on the island of Saaremaa, you follow the signposts for Kuressaare.

We got to Kuressaare, left the bus at the bus station and proceeded to try and find our hotel. I did quite well following the map but at the end of the day I had to give in and ask someone the way. Just as well, as it was up a cobbled side street. We checked in, and as it was around 1 o'clock we thought we would have something to eat as we had missed breakfast at St Olav. Unfortunately, as Saaremaa is more of a summer venue, the hotel restaurant was not open. Out we went, and, as luck would have it, just up the road was a pub with flags outside that looked inviting, called Vana Konn – 'Old Frog'. In we went and had a lovely meal. As I went to the bar to get a drink 'Apelsin' were playing over the PA system. The barman didn't speak English so I just pointed to the air and said, "Apelsin!" He gave me a funny look and said "What?" in Estonian. I repeated myself and he gave me an even funnier look and went away shrugging and laughing as if to say, "The only two English people in Kuressare knew who Apelsin are and recognised one of their songs!"

We ate at Vana Konn that night and had a lovely relaxed night in the hotel. We forwent breakfast and had a walk around the park and to the sea and around the castle at Kuresaare, and onto the beach, instead.

All too soon it was Sunday and time to head back to the bus station for Tallinn. I am so amazed at how the trip ran like clockwork. We did not have to wait at any time for the ferry. We just drove on, disembarked from the bus and went and had a cup of coffee and a cake on the thirty-five minute ferry journey. The water was very flat calm with a lot of distant islands covered in pine forests. All very relaxing. Soon (although it was a four hour journey, it passed very quickly) we were back in Tallinn and ensconced in our favourite restaurant, the Golden Piglet Inn (*Kuldne Notsu Kõrts*). Marian had told the bus driver to tell us where to get off nearest to Old Town, so that we did not go all the way back to the bus station.

# VILJANDI

I found out from Dima that the family had lived in Viljandi, and, true to form, Marian had arranged for a visit to the Selver in that town so that we could have a look around. We went to the park above the big lake and then we went around the town, and, I didn't know it, but Dima had given Marian instructions to find the house that Mum and her family used to live in. It took a few phone calls from Marian to her father whilst walking up and down the street (thank goodness for mobile phones – it would have been a bit difficult without them, running in and out of telephone boxes, not that I actually saw any). A couple of the landmarks had changed on the map that Dima had given to Marian, but we found the house in the end and there is a photo of Ron and myself standing outside it. I suspect that the road had been cobbled in those days. It was really lovely to go and see somewhere that my mother had actually lived; how I wish I could have taken her back there.

# THE EYJAFJALLAJOKULL VOLCANO

We returned from Viljandi happy to have made this reconnection with the place. It was whilst I was going back through the hotel to our room, that I saw someone sitting in front of a computer, and I heard her exclaim something about a volcano, whilst she was looking at the Easyjet site. Of course, my ears pricked up at this and so I asked her what was happening. As we do not listen to the news or buy any English newspapers whilst in Estonia, it came as a shock when I found out that a volcano was erupting in Iceland and everyone was monitoring it as it was likely to disrupt airline flights. As everything always seems to happen to me, it was then odds on that it would affect us. At first no flights were disrupted but of course, as the wind direction changed, all European flights were eventually grounded. So, there we were, stuck in Estonia.

## THE EYJAFJALLAJOKULL VOLCANO

At first, I thought that it was great to have a few more days with relatives, but then, when it looked like it was going to be a serious delay, there were things to think about like our animals being looked after, horses, dogs cats, etc., and work of course. We then started to check the news every few hours and things looked really bad. I thought I would try and find another way to get home. There was no way of going overland as all the trains were full and there were no cars to be hired, and even then the hire companies were making a fortune as they were charging enormous sums of money to go and collect cars at whatever borders or countries people were leaving them in when they got to either a train station or ferry port. I looked at going to Finland and getting a ferry from there to Harwich. There were only two cabins left and the charge was £552 per person (talk about jumping on the bandwagon!) and so we decided to ride out the storm and hope for the best – that the volcanic cloud would dissipate enough for the planes to get back in the air again in the very near future.

Luckily, we have some very good friends where we live in the UK and they looked after all the animals for us. We did have a hotel booked for one night in England, as the plane from Estonia landed late at night and so it was a bit of a palaver to ring and alter that, but I managed to do it on my mobile. I also must say that once Easyjet were back flying again it only took me five minutes to change my booking and we were re-booked for Sunday 25th April instead of 20th April. The next problem we had was with hotel rooms, because to add to our woes there was a NATO meeting in Tallinn and all the hotels were full with delegates! We had wondered why we'd heard a helicopter circling Tallinn nonstop, until we were told that the meeting was going on

## Estonia and Equines

and that Hilary Clinton was in town – once we realised, we got used to it circling all day and night on 22nd and 23rd April. It was rather eerie, I have to say.

I looked on the Internet and there were no hotel rooms to be had anywhere in Tallinn. I asked if we could stay on in our room at St Olav but the receptionist said the hotel was already fully booked for the delegation in town. Then she said that maybe we could stay, but the hotel rate would be a lot more than we were paying at the moment. Of course, I was not happy with that and told her that I would see Eric when he came on duty. Good old Eric! He said *of course* we could stay! We would have to check every day as the hotel was very busy, but of course we could have the rate we had booked at. This was a relief, of sorts but we still had to move out of the hotel on 24th April and the only other hotel we could book in Old Town was the St Petersburg, which was close but £124 a night. Oh well, we decided we would just have to go there and blow the expense.

This time for our family meal together we had chosen Troika, a lovely Russian restaurant in the centre of Old Town Square. We had been in there once with Dima during lunchtime and so went again with Marian and Jaak on 21st April. It was very expensive but very nice.

On the 22nd April I had another eerie experience. We were in our favourite restaurant next to the St Petersburg, The Golden Piglet Inn, when a man who looked like he was from the film The Bodyguard swept in, closely guarding a very important looking lady accompanied by two other important looking men. They proceeded to sit at the table next to us. The two men were one side and the lady was the other side. She slid in first on to the bench seat and the bodyguard sat with his back to the aisle, sideways on to her. The bodyguard looked like an all-in wrestler, his head completely shaved, dressed in black with a throat microphone and an earpiece. Quite frightening really. We then guessed that he must be guarding one of the delegates. His eyes were darting everywhere and he was scrutinising everyone that came in or walked past. We were fascinated. I never did find out who she was. Every so often he would put his hand to his earpiece and speak into the mic. Something else for us to talk about when we got back home, providing the volcano kept quiet!

Next morning off we trundled with our bags to St Petersburg for our last night of luxury before travelling back to the UK and back to Devon after what should have been an eleven day holiday, but turned into an expensive sixteen day holiday!

# SAD PASSING

Marian wanted us to sample Estonia in the summer, so we decided to visit and stay during August in Viimsi, which was the nearest town to Pringi, where Dima had his country cottage. It was to be Dima's 80th birthday on 12 August 2010 and so we decided to book the flight on that day and with a bit of luck we should be able to appear as a surprise with a bottle of champagne to toast the day. As the saying goes, 'The best laid plans of mice and men...' or, in our case, 'Ann and Ron'.

All these trips were going on while, between trips, I would rush home from work and we would go straight out to see Mum whose health had really deteriorated by this time. I would tell her about our trips to Estonia and show her the photographs but nothing seemed to stir anything in her memory. She would only say, "I was born in Estonia," and "Tallinn – that's the capital of Estonia".

After our adventures in Estonia in April, we went to Crete for ten days in May. While we were there, Mum had a fall at the home she was in. I was assured that she had not broken any bones or seriously damaged herself in any way but

## SAD PASSING

she did not seem to want to get up. I asked for them to get the doctor to see her again and apparently on that day she got up and sat in the day room. The doctor said that there did not appear to be anything wrong. After that, she never got out of her bed again and she would not eat anything. It broke my heart to go and see her, knowing what she had been through and now she could only just about recognise me and she was wasting away. She had completely given up.

On 26th July at 3am my mother sadly passed away. I got the call at 06.00 on the Monday morning, and so once again I had to arrange a funeral, with no instructions. I did the best that I could and arranged a celebration of Mum's life through a Humanist ceremony. One thing I had decided, though, was that I was taking Mum back to her homeland to be with her sister. I asked Ron what he thought and he totally agreed with me. There, it was decided. The only thing that bothered me was that I was splitting Mum and Dad up. Dad's ashes are buried under the apple tree in his garden where he used to sit in the summer, but I think that he would have approved of Mum going home. We had already booked the flight to go to Estonia in August so all I had to do now was to ask if it would be okay with Dima and ask if we would be allowed to bring Mum home to bury her with her sister.

---

```
Dear Marian

I now have some sad news — Mum
passed away in the early hours of
this morning — unexpectedly but
peacefully around 3.00am.
```

## Estonia and Equines

She had been a little better when
I saw her last week, although
she did not want to eat or drink
very much. The doctor had rung me
and said that they could not find
anything wrong with her since her
fall and that she would probably
go on for months or years, but it
was like she had given up and lost
her confidence. Now I have a lot
of arrangements to make. I hope
everyone is well in Estonia.

See you soon.

Love, Ann xx

---

Dear Ann and Ron

Our deepest condolences on
your loss, she will be always
remembered. We will light a candle
for her. Even though we are not
there in person to comfort you,
we are in your heart. If you need
strength to carry on, turn to your
heart for support. It is good to
hear that the departure was calm
and

## SAD PASSING

peaceful. I think she didn't give
up, she saw there was nothing for
her to do more, pleased on the
outcome of the family.We are all
well. 'Til we meet again, then we
will talk more.

Marian and family

---

Dear Marian

Thank you for your reply - it is
very comforting. We shall bring
Mum's ashes home to Estonia in
August and if it is at all possible
we would like to be able to lay
her to rest next to her sister.
She always remembered Estonia and
talked fondly about it a lot, so we
think that she would like to come
home.

I wait to hear from you. We are
pleased that all is well with the
family and hope that Erik too is
also back 100%.

Love Ann and Ron xx

Estonia and Equines

Dear Ann,

I was at the summer cottage today,
talked with Dad about your wish
and he said that he is not against
it if you'd like to bury Astrid's
ashes next to my mother/her sister.
Dad only said that he must check
the cemetery for what official
documents they need and when we
will get the time. He will come
home tomorrow and call the office.
If I know more about it then I
will write to you tomorrow evening
again. But please send me in any
case her full name and date of
birth and death or her ID number.

My holiday is 9 - 23 August so I
wait you and Ron. We have a very
nice and hot summer this year. I
don't remember when was the last
time I could swim so much. I hope
that when you come hear the weather
is good too. Aarne starts to work
from tomorrow in my workplace to
the end of August. Dad plans to
travel Narva - Jõesuu with us like
we talked last time when you were
here. He wants to stay there 3-4
days. We plan to go 16th August
morning but I don't know how long

SAD PASSING

we are there because it depends
what is the weather, our night
place... Aarne will come with us
and he must go to work 19.08. I was
in Narva-Jõesuu thirty years ago
and my Dad ten years ago. There is
very nice beach 7 km long and in
the Soviet Union time many rich St.
Peterburg Jews and Russian officers
spent their holiday there.

I think that Tallinn and Narva-
Jõesuu are like day and night but
we will see it if we go! Dad said
that he will take photos at the
same places where he had photos
took seventy years ago :):)

Okay, I finished. Aarne checks my
letter and then I press send.

Love,

Marian

---

Dear Marian

Many thanks for your reply and
many thanks to Dima. All I know is
that Mum's name is Astrid Wallis

## Estonia and Equines

(maiden name Till). Date of birth 23rd April 1924. Date of Death 26th July 2010. She has no ID number only a National Insurance Number, which is ZP940310C. I think she was married somewhere before as she never told me but I saw her marriage certificate thirty-five years ago and saw that she was a widow and her name had been Härm so this is mentioned on her Death Certificate. I will have the Death Certificate and Cremation Certificate with me as I need them to travel with the ashes on the plane. Please let me know if you need any more information, and of course whatever money that you need I will give to you when we come to Estonia. So Aarne has you for a boss — I think that he has to behave himself.

I look forward to hearing from you.

Love Ann xx

---

Dear Ann

Dad called the cemetery office today and now we know that they want to

## SAD PASSING

look your mother Death Certificate
and Dad must give written consent
because he is a resting place
owner. So now we are unable to do
anything before you come here. Then
we must go cemetery office, will pay
cash and book the time of burial.
It pays 755.- EEK-i. I think that
this would happen next day after
you come here because Monday 16.08
we travel to Narva-Jõesuu, after
that we have national holiday, then
weekend and then I must go work
again. So I think that we book the
time on Monday 23. Aug - it is my
last holiday day. I spend the night
in Viimsi 12.08 and next morning we
come and pick you up. How long you
want to sleep? Maybe we come 11 or
12 o´clock?

Love

Marian

---

Dear Marian

Many thanks for all the work you
and Dima are doing. I can send
the certificate to you on Thursday

if that makes things easier and
quicker and you would like to book
an earlier day, and I can give you
the money when we arrive. Tomorrow
is the day of the funeral and now
all the arrangements are in place,
but I know that I shall be very
upset. I will bring the certificate
in with me and post it Special
Delivery if you want me to. I look
for your reply. We don't mind
whenever you come for us, 11 or 12
o'clock, whichever is best for you.

Many thanks again

Love Ann

---

Dear Ann

Sorry that I reply until now, but I
have long days at work now because
our Swedish partner is here and we
make lot of different hot meals for
examples to his client. Then they
will decide next week are we going
to prepare them from October. I
think that you don´t have to send
us the certificate, we will work on
it when you come here. I hope that

## SAD PASSING

the funeral went smoothly and you
were not very upset.

See you in Tallinn Viimsi hotel
Athena next week.

In the meantime be strong and hang
on.

Love,

Marian

---

Dear Marian

Thank you for your reply. I hope
you are not too tired after your
long days — you will really need
your holiday — but at least you
have plenty of work. Our figures
are not so good for next year at
the school, and so we all have to
take a cut in hours. The funeral
service was beautiful and so were
the flowers, and yes I was very
upset and so was Ron but now we are
strong again. I attach the service
so that you and Aarne can read it.
I will send Dima's card to you
today so that he gets it and please

```
give him our thanks and love.

We look forward to seeing you all
next week.

Love

Ann
```

---

## The Celebration of Mum's Life

*Music to enter: 'Radetzky March' by Johann Strauss*

We have gathered here this morning with the sad task of saying goodbye to Astrid Wallis, but we have done so in a spirit of celebration and gratitude for a life well lived.

Please be seated.

It matters that you are all here today: your presence is a testament to Astrid's life and a great comfort to others, especially to Ann and Ron. On their behalf, I would like to thank you for coming here today. A warm welcome to you all. My name is Alison Orchard. It was a privilege to conduct a funeral ceremony for Bert and the privilege is deepened today.

Astrid experienced the horrors and the atrocities of war at first hand and that, perhaps, made her question the existence of God, but remarkably, her pain and suffering did not make her self-centred or introspective. On the contrary, perhaps because of those experiences, she connected deeply with her family and friends. And now a reading to reflect that:

> A Mother's love is something
> That no one can explain,
> It is made of deep devotion
> And of sacrifice and pain.
> It is endless and unselfish
> And enduring come what may.
> For nothing can destroy it
> Or take that love away ...
> It is patient and forgiving
> when all others are forsaking,
> And it never fails or falters
> Even though the heart is breaking ...
> It believes beyond believing
> When the world around condemns,
> And it glows with all the beauty Of the rarest,
> brightest gems ...
> It is far beyond defining,
> It defies all explanation,
> And it still remains a secret
> Like the mysteries of creation ...

Astrid had faith in human spirit.

This will, therefore, be a Humanist funeral. For Humanists, the fundamental truth is that life on earth is very precious and we can treasure it and nurture it without recourse to religion. I hope our simple ceremony today reflects Astrid and, in that way, you will feel her close and be able to say your goodbyes in the peaceful, dignified spirit she would have wished.

Humanists see human existence as part of one great continuum, which is evident throughout all nature. For millions of years, life on earth has evolved, such that each one of us builds on lives that come before us and become the foundation for lives that come after us. Death is an essential dynamic in that process of progression, and, in that way, death is as natural as life.

It's natural, too, that you should feel sad today and it's important to acknowledge that this is, of course, a difficult occasion for you. Astrid has had dementia for a while and so you have been saying your goodbyes for sometime now. But that brought its own sadness to you too, and I imagine you are mourning not only for the loss of the life that was but also for the life that might have been. Perhaps your sadness is tinged with a sense of being cheated, too.

But grief is a way of healing yourself, and, whilst I would never wish to belittle how necessary that is, I offer you a thought: Astrid, who became very vulnerable in life, is now at peace, we have a sense of release for her and you don't need to be too sad on her behalf. Let's face her death with acceptance and focus on her life today because this is a precious occasion.

And now, to honour that, a short verse from the 'Thoughts of Nanoushka' which Ann chose and which we would like to offer to you as though it came from Astrid herself:

> Remember the good times,
> Remember the laughter, not the tears.
> The caring, not the anger.
> The courage and not the pain.
> Your independent heart is still at last,
> And your spirit has found peace.
> You would not want us to be sad.
> To mourn too long for those we love,
> Is self-indulgent.
> But to honour their memory with a promise,
> To live a little better for having known them,
> Gives purpose to their life,
> And some reason for their death.

I never knew Astrid in life but last week I spoke to Ann on the phone and I came to understand that Astrid was not someone to whom life dealt an easy hand. With a traumatic childhood, she survived through her strength of character, determination and happy disposition and she made a good life for herself and others.

Here is her story.

Astrid Till was born on 23rd April, 1924, in Tartu in Southern Estonia; a beautiful country covered in pine forests and with friendly people. She was the eldest child born to Johannes, a major in the Estonian Army, and his wife, Lydia and she had a sister, Maret, and brother, Allan. They lived in a big old wooden house in Viljandi, and the family kept horses and loved them; indeed, Johann was a top class show jumper. Astrid had a happy childhood, she was a good student, and was due to go to University.

But the war in Europe changed her happiness and good fortune: despite declaring neutrality, Estonia was invaded and occupied, first by the Russians and then by the Germans and it is a little known fact that losses in Estonia were higher than almost all other countries and a quarter of the population. Sadly Astrid's father was one of the casualties: he was executed in May 1942 allegedly for starting an uprising in the concentration camp.

Traumatised and fearing for their lives, one by one the rest of the family fled from their homeland and the family was scattered: Maret went to Poland, Allan to Finland and Astrid went to Germany. We can only imagine how hard life was for Astrid, as a young woman of only 18. It is wonderful, however, that through the magic of the Internet, Ann has been able to find and reconnect with her Estonian family and found such friendship with her cousin, Marian, who now lives in Tallinn.

But war and exile also brought love to Astrid. It was in Germany in 1945 that she met Bert. We cannot fail to be moved by their love story: deciding they didn't want to be apart when his return to England was due, Bert chartered a two-seater plane to get Astrid – and a crate of wine as well as her friend, Ilse - back to Croydon airport. Astrid had no money, no passport and no English, but a lot of faith in love.

Immigration rules required them to marry within six months of her arrival in Britain. Despite their haste it was an excellent marriage: they were close and loving and did everything together. The young couple settled in Bermondsey, Ann was born to complete the family and she has fond memories of happy childhood homes in Ealing and Chesham.

Astrid chose not to actively remember her past and she became a thoroughly English wife and mother. She was a brilliant cook, making the best sausage rolls and meatball stew ever, and she enjoyed entertaining Bert's colleagues and clients. Blessed with 'green fingers', she was a keen gardener and was always to be found in the spring, summer and autumn on her knees in the garden amongst the shrubs and flowers.

Astrid was – and I quote - a wonderful mother, and Ann was able to grow up supported to do what she wanted. And now a poem:

> My Mother kept a garden.
> A garden of the heart;
> She planted all the good things,
> That gave my life its start.
> She turned me to the sunshine,
> And encouraged me to dream:
> Fostering and nurturing
> The seeds of self-esteem.
> And when the winds and rains came,
> She protected me enough;
> But not too much, she knew I'd need
> To stand up strong and tough.
> Her constant good example,
> Always taught me right from wrong;
> Markers for my pathway
> To last my whole life long.
> I am my Mother's garden,
> I am her legacy.
> And I hope today she feels the love,
> Reflected back from me.

## Estonia and Equines

Ann was a great fan of horse riding – possibly inherited from her Estonian family – and her Mum encouraged her. The family enjoyed many holidays together and so it was, fed up with high-pressured job in sales, that the family moved down to Cornwall in 1967 where they ran the village stores at North Petherwin near Launceston. Despite finding it hard to make a living here, it was a good move: they enjoyed a slower pace of life and the sense of community away from big city life.

Astrid and Bert lived at Crackington Haven, Newton Abbot and Winkleigh and often used to enjoy winters abroad – renting an apartment for six months at a time – in Majorca.

Finally they settled in a mobile home on Ann and Ron's land in 1984. A very creative woman, Astrid particularly enjoyed painting scenes and landscapes in oils and some of her work is on the wall in Ann and Ron's house. She liked being close to the horses and the garden and enjoyed visits from her family.

It was a cruel twist that someone so active should have to have a hip replacement in 2000 followed by another in 2001. It seemed to set her back: she never walked without crutches, she could no longer garden and it was the start of Alzheimer's disease. Life has been tough for Astrid and those who loved her for many years now.

Another reading now:

> We cannot control the movement of time,
> Nor can we control our own destiny
> Or the destinies of those we love.
> But we can take comfort in knowing
> That those who have lived in our hearts
> Are never really gone.
> For as long as we keep them with us,
> In our thoughts,
> They will be with us always.
> For love, which is timeless,
> Never ceases to exist.

You will all have your own memories of Astrid and there's no need to put them all into words – indeed it would be an impossibility. We will now listen to some organ music. I invite you to use the opportunity to thank Astrid, remember your own special, personal memories of her and say goodbye. Those of you who wish to pray, may find this the best time.

*Organ music*

Ann will collect Astrid's ashes and they will buried with her sister's back in Estonia. We have a sense of her returning home. We all build on lives that come before us and become the foundation of lives that come after us. Astrid and her story must never be forgotten because it reminds us that all that is good in human nature can triumph over the immorality and evil in our world.

## Estonia and Equines

Thank you, everyone, for sharing in our ceremony today. Ann and Ron would be pleased for you all to join them at the Bell Inn at Parkham next for an opportunity to share more memories. Our final tribute to Astrid is a musical one, which reminds us of exile, and was indeed her favourite piece. But first our final reading for today:

> If I should go before the rest of you
> Break not a flower nor inscribe a stone
> Nor when I'm gone speak in a
> Sunday voice.
> Be the usual selves that I have known
> Weep if you must,
> Parting's hell.
> But life goes on
> So sing as well.

*Music: Hebrew Slave Song by Verdi*

# TAKING MUM HOME & ESTONIA IN THE SUMMER

In the years since the Soviet Union's fall, Tallinn has been eager to make the most of its independence. Evolution and modernisation has been key to its change, yet stark reminders of the Russian occupation remain. In one of the hotels we stayed in, KGB officers – who had made it their business to wire rooms and illicitly listen in on other people's conversations for several decades – fled on the night of the Union's collapse. They left behind two untouched rooms (now known as the 'KGB Museum') full of equipment, cigarette butts, documents and other such paraphernalia.

My cousin Marian said that even in the 1990s, she always had to carry her identity card and passport with her to show to Russian soldiers to go from Tallinn to Dima's country cottage in Pringi. I cannot imagine how that must have felt, having lived in a free country all my life. Fortunately, Marian's boys have only known a free life. When Marian was small she

## Estonia and Equines

had to go on every Soviet march dressed in red with a sickle and hammer headband. She did show me some photographs of herself and Katrin her best friend. Quite unbelievable, as at that age at primary school, they would not have known what it was all about.

So this was going to be an all-new experience in more ways than one. I was looking forward to seeing Estonia in the summer as Mum had told me that it could get very hot and I had only seen it in the winter and spring, which I absolutely loved. I was really pleased that I was taking Mum back to her beloved Estonia; I only wished that I could have done that in life, but we can't have everything. I knew that I was going to be really upset later. Emotions!

We had the urn with Mum's ashes in and I looked up all the regulations for Easyjet about taking it onboard, as I did not want to fall at the last hurdle. The instructions were that it had to be taken in the cabin of the plane and not in the hold or in a suitcase. Well, we arrived at check-in and I told the guy at the desk what was in the package and he said, "Oh, I'm not sure about that," and my heart sank. I told him the regulations but he was not happy and left us standing there for ten minutes while he disappeared through a door to "speak to his supervisor". He came back and I waited with baited breath, but all was well. Our luggage was checked-in and we were left with our hand luggage and Mum's urn, which we were told we would have to declare at security again and duly did.

At last we were through and on our way to an airport lounge. Every sad situation has its humour, though. Ron turned to me and said, "I can honestly say that this is the first time I've had your mother under control!" which made me laugh because Mum was a free spirit like myself and usually did the opposite to anything anyone told her, which, of course, was a lot worse when she lived with us and suffered with dementia. In fact, it was not really my mother, as I knew her, who was living with us and that was the only way I could deal with the situation without getting too upset.

Everything seemed to be going very smoothly on this trip, although I have found that in life you can't have everything, and in this case, there was no bar on the plane, and I do need vodka to steady my nerves. When questioned, the staff said was it was due to a technical fault, and that's the only explanation we had. We took off on time (which in this day and age is something) and were an hour and a quarter into the flight when the 'Ann and Ron gremlins' struck again.

First of all, the chief of the cabin crew was called into the flight deck and disappeared for a while then reappeared and went to the back of the cabin. The pilot came on and said that we were having to turn round and go back to Stansted Airport. Oh my God, my worst nightmare, and on a plane with no alcohol too! My fear was made worse by the fact that we were not told what exactly was wrong with the plane or what was going to happen when we got back to the airport. That was my plans up the Swanee, then! No surprise for my uncle on his birthday.

Somehow or other I kept myself from falling apart and breathed a sigh of relief when we had reached *terra firma* in one piece. Once we had landed, the captain came out and told us that one of the landing computers had developed a fault and it was not safe to fly on with only one computer, (good job I did not know that before, I suppose, as we still had to land whether it was to be in Stansted or Tallinn) and that two of the three ice probes in the belly of the plane had also failed. So there we sat on the tarmac, and sat, and sat, and sat...

Nobody seemed to know what was happening, even the pilots. Apparently there were three options. One: they would repair the plane that we were on. Two: we would be offloaded and spend the night in a hotel. Three: they would try to rustle up another plane. Well, after sitting there for two hours it was decided that we were going to be put on another plane. We had the same flight crew but our cabin crew changed. And, joy of joys, there was a bar. So, we took off again and had an uneventful (thank goodness) flight to Tallinn. The main thing was that we arrived safely, albeit five hours later than expected.

This time we were staying at the Hotel Athena in Viimsi. I was a bit worried that they might not be open but they had a twenty-four hour reception. The outer door was locked, but luckily the receptionist was behind the desk so saw us, and came and let us in – and so we soon fell into bed.

We awoke the next morning to a fabulous day. It was very hot. Marian and Dima were collecting us at 11am to go to the cemetery where we had to take all the necessary documentation, including Mum's marriage certificate (as identification I suppose). We were in with the Registrar for ages and of course I could not understand anything, but when I was asked to hand over the money that was needed, I realised then that everything was in order for us to go ahead and they would give us the date that we could go and bury Mum.

With that done, we went back to Viimsi for something to eat. Marian and Dima dropped us off at the hotel and were to pick us up again on Saturday afternoon as there was a festival taking place in the evening at the Open Air Museum by the sea, which was about a hundred yards from Dima's house.

On the Viimsi peninsula, just a thirty-minute drive away, you can visit the Museum of Coastal Folk and the Viimsi Open Air Museum, which introduce the traditional life of the coastal folk. Both are in the Pringi village.

The Museum of Coastal Folk is located in the former Viimsi schoolhouse. In 2005, the first part of the permanent exposition "Along the coastline in ancient times" was opened here. On the first floor there is a display area for introducing the history and present-day activities of coastal folk – nets, boat hoists, boats, photos, stands and a lot of pleasant sea smell. There is also the ArkRoyal gallery displaying modern art of Reiu Tüür open in the museum.

After another feast at Dima's we went to the festival at the Open Air Museum. The weather was lovely and there was a rock band playing on an outside constructed stage at 10pm. The place was crowded and everyone was having fun from, 90-year-olds to babies. We stayed for an hour and then we learnt that we were catching the last bus back to Viimsi to our hotel and that left at 11.00pm. What an experience! Marian and the boys waited with us until the bus came to put us on the right one. All the seats were full and people were standing. I didn't think the driver would stop, but he did. On we got, and, as it was a minibus, squeezed down the centre aisle. The bus set off at a rate, and we were hanging on to the straps above our head for dear life as we sailed on down the road. We couldn't move very far as we were squashed in like sardines. At the next stop some passengers got off via the back door, and somehow Ron was pushed further down the back, but I felt a tug on my sleeve and an old lady pointed to the seat next to her, so, delightedly, I sat down. Poor Ron had to remain standing and as we shot off he fell backwards tripped over the step and nearly went out the back door! I could not believe that we were still stopping and picking people up on our way back to Viimsi, but we did. Health & Safety in England would have a whale of a time. Well, anyway, we made it back to the town centre, poured ourselves off the bus and back to the hotel for a stiff drink and a laugh at what had just happened.

# NARVA-JÕESUU

On Monday morning at 9.00am we were all setting off on another adventure to Narva-Jõesuu, located on the country's northern Baltic Sea coast near the Russian border. The name of the town in Estonian and Russian means 'mouth of the Narva River'.

Thanks to its seven kilometre long white sand beach lined with pine trees – one of the best in Estonia – Narva-Jõesuu has long been a popular summer destination. In the nineteenth, and early twentieth, century it was a spa town frequented by nobility from St. Petersburg, which is less than 150 km to the east, and during the Soviet period was visited in large numbers by residents of the renamed Leningrad, particularly the Russian intelligentsia, many of whom have bought 'dachas' (summer houses) in Narva-Jõesuu or on the outskirts.

In the first ten to fifteen years after the restoration of Estonia's independence Narva-Jõesuu saw few visitors, with a large number of hotels and guest houses closing their doors and going out of business. In the last few years its resort facilities have been renovated and the number of tourists is rising, however the number of hotels is still considerably lower in comparison to the late 1980s.

Marian's little car was very well filled on the Monday morning. I was lucky because I sat in the front with Marian. Squashed into the back were Dima, Ron and Aarne. It was quite a long journey. The good thing about Estonian roads is that they are very long and mostly straight – a road system courtesy of the European Union. All I knew about this adventure was that we were staying with some long lost relations. Marian had not seen them since she was a little girl and Dima wanted to go back there because he had once lived nearby.

The weather was really hot and we arrived at about 1 o'clock. We lost our way in the beginning and ended up by a river. Dima asked someone and we got the right directions in the end. The house was not on the main road, so we wouldn't have found it anyway. When we got there we extricated ourselves from the car and Merla and Lembit our relatives, came to the gate to meet us. Estonian people are very reserved. Very polite, but very reserved, and of course they didn't speak any English. Nonetheless, though Dima and Marian had not seen them for years they greeted them very warmly and shook hands politely with us. It was nice of them to invite us to their summer house in Narva-Jõesuu, but I do remember thinking to myself, "Oh dear, it doesn't look like they really want us here".

However, it transpired later that they did not realise that I was Marian's cousin and they thought that Ron and I were just friends of theirs. Of course, this must have come into conversation fairly soon, because all of a sudden we were made a big fuss of and then started a lovely two and a half days. We were very honoured and shown to our room, which was a building in the garden which consisted of one big room with a sink and a double bed and a table chairs and some cupboards. This then led into the requisite sauna that everyone seems to have in their gardens in Estonia. This particular one was a very big sauna, and we were told that it was where the Russian nobility stayed and was the best room on the property.

The main house was fairly big, with a large living room, conservatory, a big kitchen downstairs and the bedrooms upstairs. Scandinavian style! It was a good job that we were not staying there as the bedrooms were up some very narrow stairs into the roof space and both Ron's knees and mine would not have taken the strain! Going up would not have been so bad, but I don't know how we would have managed to come down. Ron probably would have been okay as he is used to ladders as a builder, but I think that I might have struggled (well, I *know* I would have have fallen down them). There was a big 'privy' at the bottom of the garden, but a flush toilet had been fitted just outside the house. I think it used rainwater for the flush. It was fine for me but it was very narrow and even I had to slide in sideways and scrunch up against the door, so Ron had no chance! He simply used the 'privy'.

With the tour of the property over, we were called into the conservatory where a great feast had been laid on, together with one and a half litres of vodka. The good old 40% kind. Back to the old routine! We all had a small vodka to toast Maret and Astrid and then that left Lembit, Ron and myself to finish it neat (which we did), albeit over about three hours when all the old photographs were brough out to show to us. The three hours passed very quickly.

Marian then decided that she wanted to go for a swim, and, as I had been ordered to bring my swimming costume from home, I duly donned it under my trousers and blouse. Marian also took a book with her and off we trudged – it wasn't very far really, only about a hundred yards – to see the beach that I had heard so much about; seven kilometers of white sand. I wasn't disappointed. It is exactly as I saw it in a photograph, only better. We stripped off and left our belongings by a sand dune and made for the water. It was twenty-four degrees and very warm. Much warmer than I thought it was going to be. It was also very shallow and so we waded out a long way before we could swim. There were only really little ripples for waves. The only slightly off-putting thing was that the water was a brown, brackish colour and full of branches that were floating crossways with the current from the Russian border. I guess all the wood was why it was very brown. We came out dried off and went back to join everyone else.

The men had been sitting in the sun and had demolished a bottle of wine and some strong beer. We had decided that we were going to take everyone out for a meal in the evening. There was only one hotel near us so we agreed to go there at around eight o'clock. Dima and Ron decided they would like to go for a swim and so did Lembit and Merla so we all trundled off back to the beach again. After another lovely swim, we walked to one end of the beach where you could look straight across at Russia, as the mouth of the river was the border. It was hard to believe that so much war had occurred on that lovely beach with a backdrop of pines, although you could see barbed wire and derelict lookout posts on the other side.

We went back home and then got ready to go out for the evening. We went to the Narva-Jõesuu Health and Spa Hotel, though, looking at the map now it rather appears that it has had a facelift. All the Estonians had lamprey – a kind of eel delicacy, (which they insisted that I tasted, and it was revolting to me) and that was all they wanted – I had a prawn cocktail and Ron had jellied meat. Then Lembit ordered the vodka again, 40 cl at a time of 40% and we had six. They did not want any other main course so we all had a dessert of either ice cream or pancakes, or both!

As we came out of the hotel, the vodka, wine, strong beer and more vodka was beginning to have an effect on Ron. We came down the steps of the hotel and I heard a clatter behind me (it wasn't a drain pipe this time, there was not one in sight!) and poor old Ron's knee had given way (or so he said – more like his balance). Anyway, we wobbled home, and – surprise, surprise – slept like proverbial logs. After our ablutions in the morning, Ron in the privy and me in the mini-toilet, we converged for breakfast in the conservatory. And there it was, the obligatory litre of vodka in the middle of the table! I have to say that we all declined except for Lembit.

Dima wanted to show us around Narva-Jõesuu and also wanted to take photos of the places he went to when he was a boy, about seventy years previously. He had the corresponding photos with him. I must say it was very interesting trying to find the exact places and then to take our present day photos. It was really hot and humid and thundery that day. Thunder seemed to be rumbling around us all morning and afternoon. Unfortunately, that is another thing that I am scared of – lightning – but I am happy to say that I did not see any of as we were wandering around in the parkland under the big trees! We found all of Dima's childhood places and they were all virtually the same as they were when he was a boy, which to me was incredible. There was only one place that did not exist and now had a kind of Estonian McDonalds built there.

We went back to our abode in the afternoon. I was hoping to go swimming again, but, as in England, the weather had changed completely and the sea temperature was now sixteen degrees with a chilly wind blowing on the shore, so that idea was knocked on the head! I was quite happy as I was definitely feeling a bit weary and so I had a little read and a snooze. (Ron just did the snoozing bit!) We were having a barbecue in the evening, courtesy of Lembit. I am not usually a lover of barbecues, but I thoroughly enjoyed it – probably helped by accompaniment of the inevitable 40% vodka. It was a 'proper' barbecue, as Lembit started the fire in the late afternoon so that he would be cooking over embers. The meat was lovely, but the only thing to spoil the event was the mosquitoes. I have never seen such big ones, and there were hundreds of them. The thunder started rumbling again and then it stopped and we had lightning for the rest of the evening but at least it didn't rain.

After a brilliant evening with Aarne as translator, we retired to bed and woke up to torrential rain, together with the thunder and lightning. Ron needed to go to the loo so he went to the outside privy and got soaking wet, but there was no way I was going out in that weather so I had to 'hang on' until it got light and the weather calmed down.

Ron and I had decided that we would go down to the supermarket that we had passed the day before, to get some vodka and beer to try and repay some of our hosts' hospitality, so we were up before anyone else and set off down the road.

It took us about fifteen minutes to walk there and to our relief it was open. We had a look around and found what we wanted and put it in the basket. All of a sudden a checkout girl came running across to us and started talking to us avidly in Russian, which of course we did not understand. We stood there looking fairly dim. (No one around could speak English or Estonian and Narva-Jõesuu is populated mostly by Russians). We tried to walk to the checkout but by this time we had two girls gesticulating and shouting at us. At least the second girl had a bit more about her and beckoned us to follow her to a notice – which of course I couldn't read, but after a while the penny dropped: they still had licensing laws there. The only thing that I could understand was one number: ten. I then deduced that we could not purchase any alcohol until that time. Oh dear, that was about two hours away, so, we had to walk back – uphill – to Merla and Lembit's house and then come down later. Marian confirmed that, indeed, in Estonia you could not purchase alcohol until after ten in the morning and so we went back later and purchased our goods with which Merla and Lembit were delighted (though maybe it would only last him one day).

At about 11am we said our fond farewells to our long-lost relatives, and piled back into Marian's car and went on to Narva as Marian and Dima wanted to show us the border there. We found somewhere to park and I could not believe the queues – firstly of people on foot on the Estonian side all shuffling through a small sort of building, and secondly of cars, trucks and lorries, queued on both sides of the border. There was a nine-foot-high chain-link fence with rolled barbwire on the top separating the town side from the road that was apparently the Russian side. It was horrible to look at and the guards were all toting machine guns – looking in cars, checking boots and lifting bonnets, just like something out of a war film, while on both sides there were lovely buildings and scenery.

After we had stood for a while and watched all the traffic passing through checkpoint, we went for a walk through a nearby castle grounds and stood marvelling at the fact that we were looking across the border (the river) at Russia – and how beautiful it was; how lovely that all the buildings had been so well preserved (it appears to be one thing about the Baltic countries: that they are so proud of their buildings). We trudged back to the car and piled in again to begin the long journey back to Viimsi.

The weather in the ensuing days was very similar to England: one day scorching hot and the next day chilly and rainy. We were enjoying our hotel in the country (well, on the outskirts of the town, but in the country compared to Tallinn). When I had chosen it (not that there were many to choose from) the blurb said it was a four-minute walk from the sea, so one hot morning we asked reception which way to go to get there and off we set. As it happens, major road improvements were going on in Viimsi and we took what turned out to be the long way round as the road was not yet open. We did find the short way back and it probably was only about ten minutes in all. But, what a lovely beach! It was white sand and totally deserted. The sea was flat calm and there was a backdrop of the pine trees. The shoreline was very different though with a lot of small rocks, and I should think it is very difficult to go for a swim as the water is also very shallow.

The following weekend, Marian's best friend Katrin and her parents, invited us to their summerhouse, which was about forty kilometres outside of Tallinn. Marian's husband,

Jaak, drove the car out there. Once again I was favoured with the front passenger seat, with Ron, Marian and Marian's son Erik in the back. We went a fair way down the main road and turned off into the countryside. After a while we came to a gated drive, which we went down, and about quarter of a mile in was the summerhouse. There were a lot of summerhouses in what can only be described as a compound. Nonetheless, it was lovely and quiet, and the house was very Scandinavian-looking, and made of wood. They have two cats – both white – just like our white one at home. When in Tallinn they live on the 13th floor of a tower block and the cats don't go out – but they love coming to the summerhouse from May to October. We met Marian's mother and father who were, similarly to all the Estonians I have met, wonderful people, who made us most welcome. Marian's father kept bringing me fruit – blackberries, wild strawberries and apricots, etc. It was a lovely day and we spent most of it outside in the sunshine in the garden.

Then came (yes, you've guessed it) a fantastic spread, together with the obligatory vodkas, and Katrin had also made one of her special cheesecakes. Katrin's father spent the rest of the afternoon with Jaak in the gazebo (I think they were putting the world to rights), and we went for a walk in the countryside. Soon our time came to an end and we were saying our goodbyes and preparing to go back to Tallinn. Katrin's father presented me with my last piece of fruit – an apple from the orchard – which I munched on the way home. What a lovely day. More lovely people, that we've been privileged to meet in my mother's homeland.

On our return to our temporary home, we made the most of the weather and walked down to the beach on several warm days. I sunbathed on the seats there and enjoyed the views. Our days were spent in this leisurely manner, and going to see Dima. Then, we had word that we could bury Mum's ashes on 23rd August.

We bought flowers and candles for Mum and her sister, and Marian and Dima collected us from the hotel so we could all travel to the cemetery together. The gravedigger arrived in the middle of the forest on his pushbike and proceeded to dig the small hole. We buried Mum's ashes and said our prayers, tidied up the grave and then Marian asked if we would like to put a gravestone there.

I was delighted and so she took us to the monumental mason's yard where we chose a lovely pink marble head stone.

And so, after all these adventures and family gatherings, we flew home again after the new experience of summer in Estonia.

# 2011 – PARNU AND MUSICAL

Our trip in 2011 was very nice again. I prefer the colder weather so this time we visited in March, and as well as doing the norm at Dima's, and going to visit the cemetery, Marian arranged a trip with Hugo and Katrin to Parnu, which is the Estonian summer capital. Firstly, we visited two Selver supermarkets, and while Marian and Katrin did whatever it was they had to do, there are so many parks in Estonia that we took the opportunity to wander through the one in Parnu by the sea and then down to the beach. How weird it was to see sand covered in snow. We found a restaurant that the girls had heard was good and had a fantastic meal there before our trip back to Tallinn. When Marian dropped us off back at the hotel, she told us that we were going to a musical the next night. The theatre was about thirty yards from the front door of our hotel and we had walked past it so many times, but we had no idea that it was a theatre. The outside was the facade of the old building but inside, it was quite modern, even to the point of having Skype in the foyer!

The musical was fantastic, and although we could not understand the words, we got the gist of the story and Marian would whisper to me every so often to tell me what was going on. The singing was delightful and the acrobatics were out of this world; how they managed to manoeuvre on such a tiny stage, I do not know. One thing I have discovered is that Estonians love their literature. Marian makes many trips to the theatre, and indeed her son Aarne is very theatrical, often appearing in plays, teaching drama and just recently, appearing in an advert on the television. I suspect that he will be something big in the drama world in years to come as he is only 23-years-old.

Afterwards, we went out for our usual family meal together and flew home to make plans for our visit the next year.

# MORE UNEXPECTED BAD NEWS

Dear Ann and Ron

I write these words in sorrow, because Jaak has passed away. In July, after his birthday, he had stomach aches and a little fever, and some days nausea. I finally told him to go to the doctors and on 25.07 and he did. The next day 26.07, they put him in the hospital and the first tests showed it was serious.Friday 29.07 after the tests the doctor told me that Jaak is very ill - 2/3rds of his stomach is full of cancersand the liver is very damaged and full of 'endorsments'.

## Estonia and Equines

It all sounded very unbelievable, because until then Jaak had no complaints about that or pain. Maybe in the spring, when he was more tired than usually. 02.08 he had been transferred to another hospital to see an oncologist, who had to determine can there be anything done or not. The verdict was there is no oncological treatment and he got taken back to the first hospital. The doctor thought we should book a place in the maintenance hospital.

Before that Jaak didn't allow to tell anyone about this - especially his mother. Tuesday evening 02.08 I told Jaak's parents and my children, that he is dying. His condition worsened in hours not days. I promised him that on Friday 05.08 I'll bring him home for the weekend, but the condition got so bad that they put him in the intensive ward. On Friday 05.08 we went to see him in the hospital and saying our good-byes. Erik was the only one who refused to come. He told that he couldn't bear to see his father suffer. Doctor thought that he won't see the coming day.

## MORE UNEXPECTED BAD NEWS

I went to look at him with Jaak's mother on Saturday 06.08 at 16.00 and on 17.55 he passed away in our presence

Jaak's mother held out well, I gave her sedatives and she told that she felt better to see her son before he passed. Dima found out few days before the passing, that Jaak is not doing well — nobody believed it would happen so quickly. I'm still in shock and I can't accept that he is gone. The analyses showed it was the doing of a very aggressive cancer cell - signet ring cell.

Jaak passed away on 06.08 and my holiday started at Monday 08.08 The first week I planned the funeral and the second one I did the paperwork and went to Haapsalu with Kadi to get away a bit. The funeral was held on 11.08 and everything was very beautiful. I ordered a pianist to play Jaak's favourite songs - Frank Sinatra, Louis Armstrong and Tom Jones. Commemoration was held in the botanical gardens 'Winter Garden'.

## Estonia and Equines

We are (me and my sons) visiting Jaak's parents every week now and also Dima. Dima's health is also not good — last two weeks he has complained about not feeling well. I want him to see the doctor this week - having hard time breathing and a swollen leg. I'm going to work again and it's still an asylum here. The good of it is that I don't have time to think about my worries.

Yesterday I went with Dima to the cemetery and booked the burial of Jaak's urn. We will do it on the day of my mothers passing in 08.09 Light a candle in memory and think of us.

I hope your vacation was better than the one in spring and you are all healthy and well. Me and Katrin are going to Turkey for a week in 25.09 - just to get away from it all. Katrin is having a hard time also - she had her gallstones removed and her father's health is still bad. Her father was in the hospital the same time Jaak was - one on the 8th floor and the other on the 7th. Every day after work

## MORE UNEXPECTED BAD NEWS

we went together to the hospital.
We both need a rest in a different
environment for a while. I just
hope that my father and Jaak's
parents hold on for at least a
couple of years.

Love,

Marian

---

Dear Marian

We were so very sad to get your
devastating news and still cannot
believe it. It happened so quickly.
I have only just found you all and
now I have lost Maret and Jaak.

We hope that Jaak did not suffer
too much, and that his mother is
bearing up. We have done nothing
but think about you since we
received your email. I have sent
some flowers to reach you on 7th
September and hope that you will
light a candle on our behalf for
both Maret and Jaak in Estonia on
the 8th, and we will do the same
here.

```
Please pass our best wishes on to
Kadi.

All is bad news - I hope that Dima
has been to the doctor and also
that Katrin and her father have
made some improvement. Please keep
in touch about Dima's health as we
worry about him. Our holiday was
very nice and the weather was good
this time. I hope that you and
Katrin have a good break in Turkey
as you both need it.

Thinking about you and sending all
our love to you, Aarne, Erik and
Dima.

I will write again soon

Love Ann and Ron
```

Sadly Jaak's father passed away as well soon after Jaak. Kadi is Jaak's daughter by his first marriage and it was nice that Marian could go away for a few days with her, and then:

## MORE UNEXPECTED BAD NEWS

Dear Marian

How are you?

Very busy I suspect. I am having a nice quiet week as all the students are away on half term and I can get on with a lot more work without being interrupted. Your new food sounds really nice - duck and pate - we shall have to fly on that airline! I have sent a little present to Dima and a letter in my poor eesti keelt! I hope that he understands it.

I hope that his health is okay and the doctor is pleased with him. Ron has not been good for the last three weeks as he has broken a bone in his foot and cannot walk very well! So now he has a bad knee one side and a broken foot the other.

He has not been to work for the last three weeks and just about manages to clean out the stables! It is slowly getting better. He can walk a bit better but if he starts doing too much it starts aching and hurting again.

## Estonia and Equines

We hope that Erik had a good holiday in Turkey. We are looking forward to coming to see you again and counting the months - only five I think now. We have had an awful week of weather with rain and gale force winds every day but the forecast is for a nice weekend - so I am looking forward to that as I can go riding and not get soaking wet! My friend's husband is very ill with pancreatic cancer and is now in hospital so that is not a very good time for her and we feel so helpless.

Well, you know that our thoughts are with you, Erik and Aarne.

Please give our warm wishes to Katrin and her family and we hope that her father is making a recovery.

Kõigi meie armastus

Ann ja Ron

## MORE UNEXPECTED BAD NEWS

Dear Ann

Thank you for the letter. I just thought of writing to you about our happenings.

Erik's vacation went well, he liked Turkey. Though it rained and hailed, one day Erik even had fever. But that didn't stop him from swimming and diving. He is having a school holiday now. In remorse I have to say that Katrin's father is dead. It happened last week, on Wednesday 19.10. They moved from summer cottage to town on the weekend and father had a little fever. Katrin's mom thought it was pneumonia and called the doctor. When the doctor arrived, father started feeling worse, blood pressure was high and they decided to take him to the hospital. In the ambulance he had a clinical death and they reanimated him. Katrin wanted to go visit him on Wednesday evening but he had died at night. Funeral was held at Friday 21.10.

Early Saturday morning we flew to Milano with Katrin on our business trip - it was planned for a long time. We had to attend a fair and visit our partner's factories, which provide us with packing machines and materials. Trip was exhausting - Milano is very populated, prices were in the space and the program was dense. We came back on Tuesday night 26.10 and went to work in the morning. Yesterday I went to our summerhouse in Pringi with Dima, to rake leaves and pick last apples. Father's health is not well - walks ten meters and already head is spinning and tired. Also complains of weakness. I hope he still hold on for the analysis on 04.11.

Today we visited Jaak's grave with Jaak's mother and Kadi - we tidied and lit candles for Jaak, my mother and Astrid. I know you thinking about us and it will be great to see you again in Tallinn. I hope Ron's leg heals and he won't break more bones.

We'll write and I hope I don't have to bring bad news again.

PS! Dima sends his best.Marian, Erik, Aarne

## MORE UNEXPECTED BAD NEWS

Dear Marian

Thank you for your letter. I am almost frightened to open the emails now as it is always bad news. We were so very upset to hear about Katrin's father. We had such a lovely time at the summer house August last year and I will always remember him bringing me all the different fruits!

Please give Katrin and her family our best wishes, love and express our sorrow.

I hope that you have recovered from your trip. It is just calming down here. One of the drivers that I use forgot to go and collect four students from Exeter airport last Sunday for the start of term and everyone said it was my fault, but I have only just found out that he cannot read and write much, so I will have to be very careful when I ask him to do things for me or just give him written details which I did the week before!

How is Dima? We were very worried to hear that he cannot do much

> without feeling giddy and weak. You
> said he was going to the doctor on
> 4th November - so we hope and pray
> the news is not too bad.
>
> Thank you for lighting a candle for
> Mum — we really appreciate it as
> she is so far away!
>
> Ron is gradually getting better
> and went to work yesterday for a
> few hours. It starts to hurt again
> if he does too much on his foot.
> We look forward to hearing about
> Dima's health, although I shall be
> frightened to open it!
>
> Love to you Erik, Aarne and Dima
>
> kõik meie armastus
>
> Ann and Ron

And so it was that we received the news that Katrin had lost her father too. What a positively awful year!

# 2012

In March 2012, we set off to Tallinn again. The flight was bang on time and we arrived at St Olav Hotel for the fourth time. I was sorry that the manager Erik was not there any longer as he was always very helpful and gave us a good price, and this time the hotel was 20% dearer. We had our usual meal in the Golden Piglet Inn and retired for the night. In the morning at about 7am I could hear dripping and noticed water coming off the ceiling above the window. I thought it was raining outside but it was not – nonetheless, half an hour later the water was running down the curtain and so I moved our suitcase and some clothes onto a chair away from the window, both of which were getting rather wet!

  We went for breakfast and stopped off at reception to explain what was going on in our room. The female receptionist obviously thought that we were making 'much ado about nothing', but said that she would report it to the caretaker. After our breakfast and upon our return to the room what a sight met our eyes. Everything was awash! In actual fact it was very dangerous. The water was pouring out of the bathroom ceiling and the floor was three inches deep in water. The water had spread across the ceiling and was pouring over presents that I had brought with me, which I thought that I had moved out of harm's way onto the dressing table on the other side of the room. Ron and I charged back to reception and finally got across to her the severity of the situation. She gave us a key to another room that we could use.

When the caretaker arrived he did see how dangerous it was and tore around turning of the electricity. We then had to paddle in and out rescuing our clothes, presents and items that we had distributed around the room, whilst the cleaners were mopping up and stripping the bed etc. around us. We were never offered another room or so much as an apology, and so we had to stay in a tiny room without even a wardrobe for two weeks. It is their hard luck as I always vote with my feet and we shall never stay there again, which is a great shame as it was a very nice, reasonably priced, centrally located hotel. We enjoyed another lovely two weeks without any mishap.

Later that year, we went to Estonia again in the summer and stayed at The Athena in Viimsi. Ron renewed all the decking at my Uncle's house as it had got very bad and he had fallen a couple of times. We were very brave and used the infamous bus to go to and from the hotel, instead of a taxi. This was not as raucous as in 2010. Marian had printed the bus timetables for us and it was very easy and cheap. We continue to look forward to our holidays in Estonia, and I always have a reason to go back: to see my Mum.

**VÄLISÕIGUSABI** **ADVOKAADIBÜROO**

*Müürivahe 41, Tallinn, Tel +(372) 644 44 11, Fax +(372) 644 51 24*
*Postal address: P.O. Box 425, Tallinn 10504, Estonia*
*www.adv.ee E-mail: mahhov@adv.ee*

August 22th 2007

Dear Mrs Ann Neale,

The money you transferred has arrived. Thank you.

Hereby I send you the translation of the text that you found about your grandfather on the internet:

Johannes-Voldemar Till was born in October 12th 1897 in Viljandimaa, Estonia. He had higher education and worked as an accountant. He was arrested in July 2th 1941 in Rakvere, Kunderi street 12, Estonia. He was sentenced to death in March 31th 1942 according to § 58-4, 58-10, 58-11 and kept in Permi oblast, Usso camp, Russia until May 8th 1942, which is the date of his execution. He was prosecuted for preparing a rebellion in the camp. J-V Till was a Major of Estonian Republic.

So far we have detected that your grandfather, Johannes-Voldemar Till's wife's name was Lidia (born in 1906). He also had an older sister named Linda Utermüller (born in 1892). Your grandparents had two daughters and a son – Maret (born in 1929), Astrid – your mother (born in 1924) and Alun (born in 1932).

J-V Till's father was named Jaan Till, he was born in 1860 and worked as a carter. His mother Maria Till, born in 1872 was a housewife.

We could also find two pictures and fingerprints of your grandfather from his imprisonment days. See the attached files.

We will let you know of any further information we find as soon as possible.

Yours truly,

Ivo Mahhov

Kairi Reiman *Reimal*

# VÄLISÕIGUSABI ADVOKAADIBÜROO

Müürivahe 41, Tallinn, Tel +(372) 644 44 11, Fax +(372) 644 51 24
Postal address: P.O. Box 425, Tallinn 10504, Estonia
www.adv.ee  E-mail: mahhov@adv.ee

17th September 2007

Dear Mrs Ann Neale,

I am pleased to inform you about the results of our researches:

Jaan Till was born on 30th of April in 1829 and died on 8th of January in 1912. He was married to Ann, who was born in 1831 and died on 20th December in 1915. They had altogether 5 children:

1. Jaan Till, who was born on 25th of March in 1860 and married to Maria Meomutel in 1889. Maria was born in 1872. Jaan and Maria Till had altogether two children:

   1.1. Linda Till, who was born in 1892, her married name was Utermüller and

   1.2 Joahnnes-Voldemar Till, your grandfather, who was born on 12th of October in 1897. He was married to Lidia, your grandmother, who was born in 1906. Johannes-Voldemar Till died on 8th of May in 1942, his wife Lidia died on 24th of April 2006.

   They had altogether three children:

   1.2.1. **Astrid Till**, your mother, born on 23rd of April in 1924,

   1.2.2. **Maret Till**, who was born on 2th February in 1929. During the WW II Maret fled to Poland to live with her aunt Linda Utemüller. Maret has been married twice, her first marriage occurred when she was only 16 year old with Viktor Kisna, with whom she lived in Poland for some years during the WW II. Maret and Viktor had one child:

   1.2.2.1. **Igor Kisna**, who was born on 30th of October in 1947, Igor is now living in Russia and has a rare contact with her mother, Igor is married but has no children,

   Maret is now living with her second husband, Dimitri Sevrjukov in Tallinn. They got married in 1966. Maret and Dimitri Sevrjukov have only one child:

   1.2.2.2 **Marian**, who was born on 8th of January in 1966, her married name is Kallas. Mariann Kallas has altogether two children:

   1.2.2.2.1. **Erich Kallas,**

   1.2.2.2.2. **Aarne Kallas,**

1.2.3. Allan Till, who was born on 16th of July in 1931. During the WW II Allan moved to Australia, married to Colleen Florence, it was second marriage for her. Allan Till, your uncle died on 25th of July in 2001 in Australia. Allan had two stepchildren:

    1.2.3.1. **Jennifer Curtis,**

    1.2.3.2. **Brian Curtis.**

2. Jaak Till, who was born on 4th of February in 1863 and died on 16th of September 1926. He was married to Ann Leita on 18th of March 1884. Ann was born on 5th of January in 1861. Jaak and Ann Till had altogether 10 children:

    2.1. Mari Leita, who was born on 1th of October in 1880. Mari's family name was changed to Till,

    2.2. Ann Till, who was born on 7th of March in 1885 and was married to Johan Tukk in 1902. Ann and Johan Tukk had altogether four children:

        2.2.1. Jaan Till, who was born on 14th of June in 1902,

        2.2.2. Maria Till, who was born on 17th of July in 1904 and married on 29th of July in 1920,

        2.2.3. died young,

        2.2.4. Hermann Johannes Till, who was born on 19th of April in 1912.

    2.3. Jaan Till, who was born on 2th of October 1887 and married to Minna in 1919,

    2.4. Liisa Till, who was born on 31th of March in 1890 and married to Mihkel Palta in 1916,

    2.5. Epp Till, who was born in 1891 and died young,

    2.6. Hans Till, who was born on 4th of January in 1893,

    2.7. Leida Rosolie Till, who was born on 12th of June in 1895,

    2.8. Ella Alvine Till, who was born on 18th of November in 1897 and was married on 26th of June in 1921,

    2.9. Helmi Johanna Till, who was born on 22th of September in 1900 and married to Johannes Tomson in 1924,

    2.10. Salme Till, died young.

3. Kadri Till, who was born on 25th of March in 1866, her married name was Ott,

4. Epp Till, who was born on 8th of September in 1871, she was married to Johannes Anderson,

5. Ann Till, who was born in 1874, she died young, unmarried and without children.

Note that the persons whose names are underlined are currently alive and possible to get in touch with.

I am sorry to inform you that your aunt Maret has also Senile Dementia. However, we had a chance to meet Maret's husband, Dimitri Sevrjukov, he and his daughter Marian are very interested in getting in touch with you. They were interested in your postal address for they have some pictures to send you of Maret and also of Allan who visited Estonia shortly before his death.

Whilst Maret and his husband do not speak English I can give you their daughters, Marian's contact. Her e-mail address is   and postal address Mustamäe tee 139-84, Tallinn 12918, Estonia. If you are interested then it is also possible to get in contact with your uncle's stepchildren in Australia, Maret's husband has the necessary contacts.

I hope the information we provided you is of any help. If there are any additional questions don't hesitate to ask.

Yours truly,

Kairi Reiman

5.10.07

Dear Ann!

It is great, that You began to look for Your relatives in Estonia. Unfortunately a bit late. But You have found alive Your ant, sister of Astrid. It was a big surprise and joy for all of us. Because Your grandmother and uncle Allan, who lived in Australia, looked for Your mother through Red Cross, but with no success. They thought that Astrid was killed at the end of the war in Germany. But Your mother found Maret through somebody, who visited Estonia in the end of 70ies. And they started to write letters to each other. After the mother died, Allan also wrote letters and Maret was so lucky, that he visited us in 2001 summer. He came with his nurse, because he had bone tuberculosis. He couldn't walk a lot, he got pains. I went to Viljandi with him and we were at the lake there and looked the house where You lived. After visiting Estonia, they traveled to Vienna and Paris. Allan wanted to see the cities. It was his first journey to Europe. These all were probably so big expressions to him, that getting home, his condition got worse and he died. If he didn't come here, he probably lived a bit longer, but he saw his sister and his home country.

I understand that Your mother is sick and she is not coming to Estonia. Maret in also not coming to You, because she is probably more sick than You mother. She has a deep depression and she had a little stroke a year ago. But You could come to us! You meet Marianne and Your home country and You can carry on writing letters. Mariann has two sons: Eerik (13) and Aarne (16). Eerik plays football and went to play to USA last summer. They were invited by a Minnesota club. Our boys were there for 2 weeks.

We live in a new district in Tallinn with Maret. Mariann lives nearby with her family. But in summer we go to our summer house. It is 20 kilometers from Tallinn at the sea. If You come, You will see.

I send some photos, I will send some more later. Maret has some photos from Your childhood.

That is all for the first time. Maret is in the hospital now, but she kisses and sends regards to You.

Dima.

P.S. Maret come to home from hospital at 10.10.07 Dima.

Maret 30 Years Old

Uncle Dima and Aunt Maret

Allan and Maret

Ron and I under the TARVAS in Rakvere

Mum's old house in Viljandi

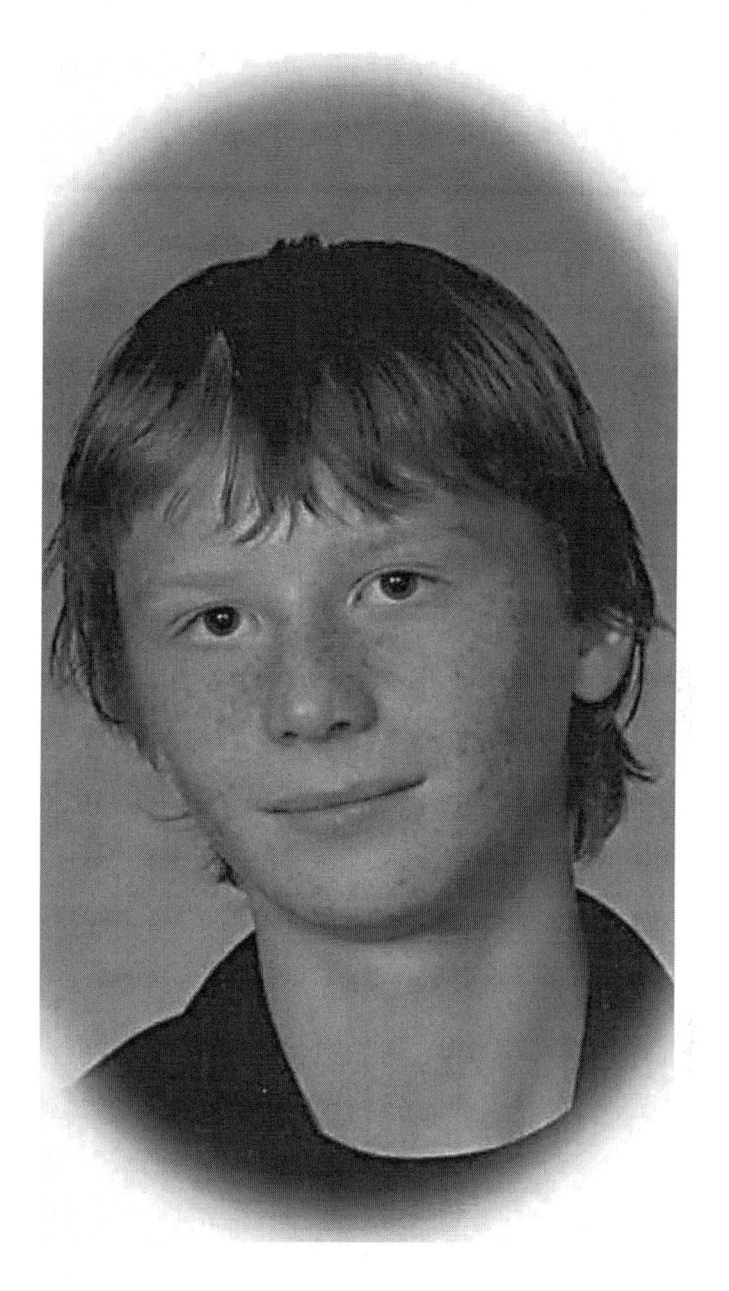

Aarne, my cousin's eldest son

Winter in Estonia

Ron, Katrin's father, Jaak and Erik

Our visit to Katrin's parents' Summer House (Ron, Marian, Katrin)

Laying Mum to rest with her sister in her homeland

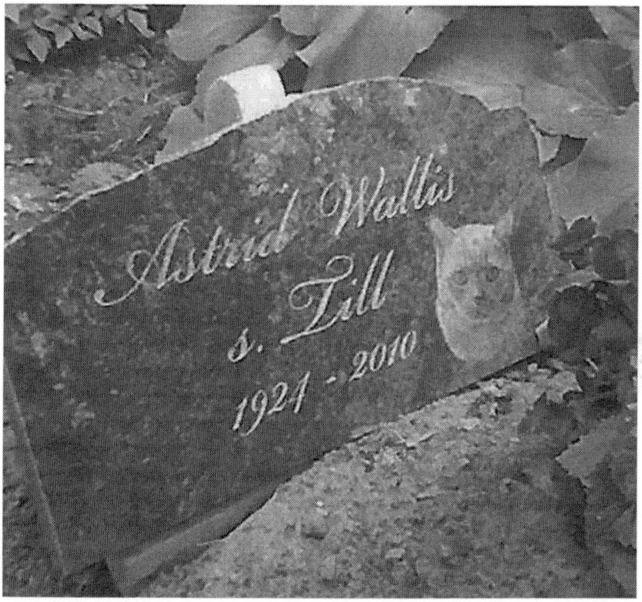
Astrid Wallis
s. Till
1924 - 2010

# PART TWO
MY HORSES

Grandfather jumping in Estonia in 1927

Practising jumping on my beloved Music in Amersham, 1962

Ringo at Penn Horse Show 1967

# A STUBBORN INHERITANCE

I think I must have inherited my grandfather's stubbornness, and this trait first reared its ugly head when I had toothache and I was taken to the dentist – Mr Williamson – I shall never forget it. I was eight years old, and you can imagine what dentists were like in 1956!

He took one look and said that the offending tooth would have to come out. When we lived in Ealing I had had two teeth taken out at a dentist there, and I was held down in a chair with this awful rubber mask smacked over my mouth and nose and the horrendous feeling of pins and needles every where as I slipped into unconsciousness, surrounded by the revolting smell of rubber – and obviously this bad experience coloured my opinion of dentists. There was no way that I was having *that* done again, so I said as much to the dentist. They tried to get me out of the chair but I wouldn't budge and got hysterical. They sent Mum back out to the waiting room and then proceeded to try and prise me from the seat. I am glad to say it took all three of them. I think

Johannes Voldemar Till would have been proud (although at that time I was entirely unaware of him ever having existed)! The dentist, his nurse, and then the anaesthetist manhandled me down a corridor, held me down in yet another chair and slapped the revolting rubber mask on again. Of course, afterwards I was okay, but how things have changed. The practice would be sued for assault these days. What a way to treat a child and expect them to go the dentist willingly!

    A few weeks later, Mum took me to the hairdresser to have my hair trimmed and when we came out she said, "Oh, by the way you have to go to the dentist for a check up, and your appointment is now." That was it. I ran off and kept twenty yards in front of poor Mum all the way home. All you could hear was Mum saying "Ann, come here! Ann, come here!" but 'No way, Pedro' (to quote Del Boy) – I was never going to darken his doorstep, and I think Mum knew it was no use. I didn't go to the dentist again until I was about twelve years-old, by which time Mum had heard some horrid things about Mr Williamson and so even she changed her dentist to Mr Pritchard. I did consent to see him and although he seemed quite nice he did have a warped sense of humour, as I suppose you would call it! If I needed a filling and he said would you like it done now or later, whatever I said, he always do the opposite. But at least I was treated like a human being.

# EARLY EQUINE YEARS

Before I started riding properly, I also used to go to tap and ballet lessons, which I loved. When we lived in Ealing I used to go to lessons there, I suppose from about the age of 6. The lessons were every Saturday morning and they led to a couple of shows each year, which I thoroughly enjoyed. I also loved playing the piano, which I know I got from Mum because I knew that she was a good pianist in her younger days. Dad happened to mention it to my dance teacher, and her husband, who always played the piano for the classes, said that he would be happy to give me lessons as he was a qualified teacher. So, every Wednesday evening we used to go their house and Dad would deposit me there, and go and sit and wait for me in the car. I had the lessons for about a year and Dad bought me piano to have at home. I remember one evening when I was having my piano lesson, there was a terrible thunderstorm – which you now know I am petrified of – and they had a dog who was also petrified. She spent the whole of my lesson huddled under the piano against my legs, shaking like a jelly. Somehow or other we both got through the lesson.

## Estonia and Equines

After a year, my teacher became unwell and did not play for our dance classes. I was told that he had 'flu and I remember going to visit him at his home when he was in bed – he looked awful. It turned out that he had leukemia and nobody wanted to tell me. Obviously there were no cures for cancer in the 50s and sadly he passed away. Unfortunately that was also the end of my piano lessons. I was so upset that I didn't want anyone else to teach me. Of course I regret it now, but things are easier to see in hindsight. I gave dancing up as well, and then my only hobby was riding. Firstly, at the farm in Cholesbury and then, later, with Music.

We always used to go to Bude in North Cornwall for our holidays, and of course I was mad on horses so I used to spend all day with the beach ponies: it's funny how something so simple could keep people so happy. I wonder how long it is since they last had such ponies on the beach there? I expect Mum and Dad were glad to get rid of me and we would stay there all day. People would come along for a ride on the ponies and they would be led up the beach and back again. There was a skewbald pony about 13.2hh, called Sparky and a black horse about 15.2hh, called Gypsy. The lady that used to bring them from the farm every morning was called Mrs White and as I had several rides a day (I used to spend all my pocket money on them at 6d a ride). Mrs White could see that I could ride and after a couple of days, I was allowed to ride Sparky to and from the farm which was a few miles away from Summerleaze beach. I would get up early and forgo breakfast, walk down to the farm which was also a couple of miles from the boarding house that we stayed in, and then ride Sparky to the beach with Mrs White on Gypsy. It made my fortnight and it also meant that Mrs White did not have the slog of walking up and down the beach, because, of course, I did it. It kept me fit, for sure!

Because I was always on my own, Mum and Dad asked if Ann, a friend, would like to come on holiday with us the next year. We both rode the ponies then and Mrs White used to give us riding lessons at the farm. I can remember being really miffed because she said that Ann had a better seat than me and looked better on the horse!

We found another riding stable in Poughill and Mum decided that she would like to come as well, which I thought was great. I was about 11-years-old at the time, so Mum would have been 35. I rode a lovely black pony called Twinkle and they put Mum on a 15.hh pony called Punch. He was very naughty. It was quite frightening really as we went across the cliffs. We went through a gate and Mum was told to wait there while we had a canter. When we stopped, all of a sudden there was Mum galloping full speed towards us frantically trying to stop the pony. She couldn't, he swerved and she fell off. She hurt her neck and back quite badly and that was her one and only foray into riding horses with me, which was a great pity, and it really frightened her. At the end of the holiday, Ann and I went for another ride at the Poughill stables, and that same pony nearly galloped Ann over the cliff edge. She came off and fractured her coccyx. Punch was well named, as he sure did pack a punch for both Mum and Ann.

# CHOLSEBURY

I rode the ponies on the beach every time we went to Bude on holiday, and then, after a couple of years, I started riding at a farm that was eight miles away from us when we lived in Chesham. Myself and another Ann used to go every Saturday afternoon whatever the weather. I rode a variety of different ponies and horses from 12.2hh to 17.1.hh (an ex-point-to-pointer), because it seemed that I could ride anything. These were not riding school horses: they were ordinary horses and ponies on a farm, which of course was the best way to learn!

I can even remember the names and colours of them now. Tango was the smallest, a skewbald at 12hh. I did not like riding her very much as she was just like a Thelwell pony. Then there was Jane, a bay, Peter, a white grey, Mickey, a dapple grey, Tweedie, a flea-bitten grey, Brandy, another bay, Robin, a chestnut and Donna, a liver chestnut. I loved riding them as they were each completely different, but my favourite was Freckles. She was a white grey, 13.3. with a flea-bitten face, hence the name. I think Mr Thompson had bought her out of pity as she was very nervous. You could not catch her or let her out to go to the field. She had to run loose always. She was fine to groom in the stable though.

Ruth, whose family owned the farm, was the only one who used to ride her but I was asked if I would like to give her a go, and so Ruth said I could try. We set out, and I got on with her well, so I was allowed to take her out on the ride every week, as Ruth wanted to ride her own horse, Donna. The only hiccup I ever had was one Saturday afternoon we were riding across the fields and Ruth's father and workman were getting bales of hay in on the tractor and trailer. We went over and stopped to talk to them, but when the tractor engine started-up, Freckles reared-up and bolted back towards the farm. As she was so frightened I did not have a hope of stopping her.

We went flat-out through the gate, into the next field and were galloping parallel to an electric wire fence. I was a complete passenger and unfortunately the farm and her stable was situated to the right. She turned to go there, tried to jump the wire and of course it came down. Luckily we did not get tangled up in it and next we were hammering towards the wooden fence, which was quite high. I have to say that I wasn't frightened – I don't know why – I just thought. "Oh well, I have jumped her before!" and I knew that she was capable of clearing it. She started calming down as we got nearer to home and I managed to pull her up as we got to the fence, much to everyone's relief. We spent the next hour putting the electric fence back up and then we continued on our ride – luckily none the worse for our escapade – but I always steered clear of any tractors in the future.

That last story brings to mind the best piece of riding that I have ever seen in my life. I had an acquaintance at school called Linda (unfortunately I cannot bring her surname to mind). She was in another class but had a horse that was about 15.hh. Linda had her as a two-year-old, and broke her in herself. She kept her at a farm about two miles away from me and we used to go out riding together sometimes in the evening, although not that much as I had to ride along the busy A40 to get to her. My horse by then was my beloved Music who was absolutely fine in traffic, and there were big grass verges, but I still to this day do not like heavy traffic and tried to avoid it where possible. Anyway, we were at a show in Amersham at Rectory Farm and had both gone along separately (dear Music came home with six rosettes: two for jumping and four for gymkhana classes – all 1sts and 2nds). Well, Linda was jumping in the ring and all of a sudden her horse's bridle broke. The horse just ploughed on, straight through a ring fence and disappeared down over a hill out of sight. We all ran to shut any gates that were out onto the road so that we could contain what looked like it would be a horrible accident. Then, Linda appeared back over the horizon at a very sedate canter that was getting slower and slower. She was leaning forward in the saddle and had her hands over the horse's eyes. What quick thinking and presence of mind – and also a lot of nerve to do that. Of course the horse was weaving all over the place and getting slower, and we all converged so that when she actually stopped Linda could jump off and the horse could not charge off again. It was a fantastic piece of riding. I am sorry to say that when I moved to the west-country I did not keep in contact with Linda, but I have never forgotten that day.

# MUSIC

You will know how I came by my first pony as it is covered in Part 1 of this tome! Up until I was 17 and passed my driving test, Dad always used to take me up to the farm in Amersham on a Sunday morning, and if I was lucky, some of the older girls that had horses up there would allow me to go riding with them, which was great as it made me feel very grown-up. I used to take Music, a Cadbury's lemon sponge, which she loved, and a quarter of Sharps Extra Strong mints (that was the good old days when you could go into a sweet shop and buy a 'quarter' of a pound of sweets. She would not eat any other mints other than Sharps. Not Badgers or Polos as those were probably the only other two on the market in 1961). One particular Sunday we had made our stop at Elsons, the sweet shop, and gone on to the farm, but for some unknown reason, I could not catch Music. All the ponies and horses were out together in about forty acres made up of several different fields and had an uninterrupted run into each field. Music had only just gone up to the farm and obviously thought that she would have a 'high old time' with me that day. Dad and I ran and ran and kept cornering her and then she would just gallop straight through us and into the next field. After about an hour of this Dad and I had her cornered and Dad said, "We've got her now!" With that, Music charged at the hedge, which was about five feet high with a huge drop the other side – and sailed over. Dad looked at me and said, "Right! I have had enough." Even the Sharps Extra Strong mints couldn't tempt Music that day.

So off we went to the Rose & Crown pub in Chesham (which was where Dad normally went to see some friends before he came back to collect me an hour and a half later on a normal Sunday). I was really disappointed that I had not been able to go riding but I was slightly placated by being allowed in the pub, which had a piano. I was allowed to play it and also I had a drink of Ryvella, a lovely non-alcoholic Swiss drink that I don't think you can buy in this country anymore. (Actually, I have just looked it up on the Internet and the fact that you can still buy it amazes me, although like most things, it has had to keep up with the times: you can get a low calorie version now!) I can't really remember how I did it but I worked out my own way of catching the mare and although she never tried me out again, I was the only person that she would let catch her, especially in a large area.

When I got married, I still had my beloved pony Music. When we bought her, she had been advertised as a seven-year-old, and not knowing any different we presumed that she was. When I went to the farm in Amersham, Mr Clarke who owned the farm and who was an absolutely wonderful help and so kind to me, had a look at her teeth and gave me the bad news. He could not say exactly how old she was but she was definitely over twenty! I was devastated (I was thirteen at the time) but I wasn't to know how long-lived she would be.

I was so lucky that when we moved to North Petherwin in the west-country in 1963, I still had Music. Dad had got tired of driving to Shepherds Bush every day from Chesham and then over to his other factory in Iver, so he relinquished his Directorship and bought the Post Office Stores in North Cornwall. I was lucky enough to have another horse, a big bay heavyweight, bought for me by Dad in 1966. His name was Ringo; very 'a la mode' for the time with the Beatles being so popular. He had been South Bucks Riding Club Champion in 1965 and as such Dad thought that I would 'go places' with him. How wrong can you be! I never really got on with him. He had a nice temperament to handle but to ride was a completely different story. He used to suddenly take off and buck like "funno" (an expression I once heard and liked the sound of). I never really got to the bottom of him. I rode him quite a lot in the four years that I had him but never felt comfortable.

We lived in North Cornwall for three years and in due course, I sold Ringo – then it was just me and Music again. Nobody would ever ride her – well, not more than once anyway – because they always fell off, except for one person who got galloped away with! Linda at the riding farm in Cholesbury, my friend Ann, another friend of mine Penny and one person in North Petherwin who thought she could ride, all rode Music just the once! It got to the stage that I dared not let anyone else ride her at all. I, of course, loved her to pieces. And so, I still had dear Music when I got married, so she must have been around 31 or 32-years-old. When I got married, it was 'love me – love my horse', and luckily for me my husband-to-be did share my love of horses. He found a little plot of land in the village of Langtree where we were to live in an end terrace cottage and turned a shed in the bottom of the garden into a lovely big stable for Music. That brings me to a story that even I don't believe.

# RSPCA

One horribly cold, dark, wet and windy night there was a knock at the door and when I opened it there was a big man in a black uniform standing there. Our street did not have any lighting, so I had no idea who it could be. He asked if he could come in, and of course he did. He was from the RSPCA and had been told that I was keeping an old pony – with no teeth – out in the middle of Langtree Moor in all weathers with no shelter. I was absolutely flabbergasted as there is no bigger animal lover than me! Ron was down in the stable at the bottom of the garden and I shouted to him to come to the kitchen. The Inspector asked if there was any chance of seeing the pony and of course Ron said, "Yes". "Do I need my wellingtons?" asked the Inspector. "I shouldn't think so," said Ron, switching the light back on for the stable that he had turned off when he came in. "Oh," said the Inspector, "isn't the pony out on the moor in all weathers?" "Follow me," said Ron, and I brought up the rear. We walked towards the light at the bottom of the garden and opened the door and inside was a lovely contented pony – up to her belly in straw – with a manger full of oats and swedes, a rack full of hay and "shining like a shilling" as they say in the westcountry! (Ron had just given her the usual evening grooming session) "Do you have any other horses?" asked the man. "Oh no, only this one," I said. "I am very sorry to have bothered you," was his reply. He would not tell me who had reported the fact that I was keeping a pony in poor conditions. He thought perhaps it was a jealous person in the village who would have liked a pony but did not have one. Although it was a horrible experience, I am glad that at least someone had bothered to check on the report.

# HUNTING

I used to ride Music in the afternoons and sometimes at weekends. I have never been fond of hunting but the Stevenstone Hunt was meeting at the Green Dragon pub in Langtree and as Ron was a 'hunty' person and wanted me to go, I thought I ought to, to please him as he helped to look after Music, getting her food, straw, hay etc. through his farm connections – him being a builder and 'in' with everybody. Ron disappeared one evening with Music on a halter having said he was going down to see his friend Dave in the village. Dave also liked horses and hunting, indeed, when we first moved into the village, Dave used to borrow our car because he didn't have one, and Music (very occasionally), to go hunting on because he didn't have a horse! Anyway, when Ron and Music returned I was in tears. They had clipped her off, all bar a saddle patch, and she had never looked so lovely! I couldn't wait now until Saturday so that I could go to the meet and show off my beautiful pony who looked nothing like her 33 years. I set about cleaning my tack with a vengeance.

Saturday arrived and I didn't have to do much grooming. I tacked-up and went up to the pub where the Hunt was meeting. I felt a million dollars, as normally in the winter, poor Music was just in her woolly winter coat. Music and I hung around for quite a while and Ron came up to see us, and was also proud of Music. She was very good, standing in the small field at the meet, and then we moved off.

Oh my god! From the moment we moved away, she cantered on the spot the whole time. We went a fair way through fields, along roads and she cantered all the way. I had her in a Pelham bit with double reins and she was pulling my arms out! I lasted for about two hours. The only time she stopped was in the middle of Langtree moor as we followed the huntsmen out through the corner of a field that became really boggy, until Music had had enough and jumped over it! I then decided that *I* had had enough and left with another girl back to Stibb Cross, where I said my farewells to her, turned right and headed on home to Langtree. When I got home I fed Music and bedded her down for the night. I was getting stiffer and stiffer (I was only about 23 but I had never had a ride like that). I flopped in an armchair and that was it; I did not have the energy to get my boots off so that's where I was when Ron came home later. He pulled my boots off for me and I went to bed! The next day I could hardly walk and I definitely couldn't sit down!

# LOSING MY BELOVED FIRST PONY

Inevitably, the awful day finally came when I lost my beloved pony. She had been going lame after riding a little way down the road, and it got so that I could not lead her twenty yards down the road because she just got so terribly lame. I had the blacksmith come to see her. He took her shoe off but could not find anything wrong. It was obvious that I could not just keep her standing in the stable and as she was now around 34-years-old, there was an awful decision to make. Ron said that he would arrange everything for me as I said that I did not want to know. I was at a computer course in the Barnstaple Motel, but somehow I knew what was happening, and when I got home, I found out that I had been right. Ron had gone with her and arranged for her to go to the kennels, where she was put down. She had walked up the ramp of the lorry and thought she was going to a show or hunting. Ron inspected her leg afterwards and found out that she had a spur of bone that had either grown or split in her leg and that was what was making her lame, and of course the right decision had been made because there was nothing that could have been done for her. Certainly not back in 1972. So there I was now horseless!

At that time, I worked in Toy Works Limited in Bideford and used to go home every lunchtime with my friend Cathy Davidson. They had a guesthouse in Northam that had stables attached, which they rented out. They also had a few acres behind the house, albeit very steep ground. Ian, Cathy's husband, decided that he would like to take up riding as they had the facilities to hand and he was offered a horse called December, a piebald. As they had no idea about horses they asked Ron and myself if we would go with them to see him. Well, we went to Parracombe and Embers (as he became affectionately known) was about 15.hh with the most beautiful temperament. Ian, who had not ridden before, got on very well with him, and, lucky me, I got to ride him on Saturday afternoons. If I had a day off work, another friend, Nikki, who was a colleague in the Payroll office, used to come with me and so we would hire a horse from the stables at Tadworthy and go out for a couple of hours, which was great. So there I was, catching the bug again, but Ron said that I could not have another horse as there would be nowhere to keep it (because the people that owned the land had decided to build on it), and we couldn't really afford one anyway. That was like waving a red rag at a bull! I felt my stubborn inheritance raise its head – the spirit of my granddad, Johannes Voldemar Till! I would see about that!

# L'OREAL

I saved and saved and did 'outwork' in the evenings to get some money together so that I could afford a young, unbroken horse. I also asked local people and farmers if they had anywhere I could keep a horse, and luckily, I found a small plot for 50p per week. I looked in the local paper and saw a couple of young horses advertised near Lostwithiel. Cathy said she would come with me, so unbeknownst to Ron off we went to Lostwithiel. We saw one horse that was kept in a garage, but I didn't fancy that one and then we went to Darite to see a 2-year-old dun. The name of the bungalow was Ponderosa. Very apt! Against my better judgement (as I was to discover), and because there were not many dun horses around, I decided to buy her and named her L'Oreal (because when I lived in Chesham the hair products made for L'Oreal were made by Goldens in Chesham, hence the yellow – dun – connection). Big and brave when I started out, I now had to go home and tell Ron what I had done. That was a different story. Cathy and I chain-smoked all the way home discussing how I was going to broach the subject. Oh well, I decided, there was only one way to do it – jump straight in!

Well, Ron was not too pleased – but as I had everything arranged and could counter every argument against the idea, in the end, he had no option but to let me get on with it. I then asked Ron's friend Dave if he would break her in for me, which he agreed to do for £30 (a princely sum in those days) so now I was all systems go! Another friend (had a lot of them didn't I) in the Sales office said that they would borrow a trailer and as they had a Land Rover, they would come down with me to collect L'Oreal and bring her back. I asked Ron if he would come with me as loading a youngster who had never been in a trailer before is usually a bit of job and I thought another strong pair of hands who knew what they were doing might help. Well, Ron said no, he wouldn't come and that I could get on with it myself. I was a bit upset at this, which is obviously what he wanted, but I was not going to be deterred, and waited for Nancy and her husband to arrive. When they did, Ron changed his mind at the last minute (though I think that he meant to come all along, he just wanted to make me sweat, which I did) and I was really pleased. Off we set to the Ponderosa!

We arrived at the appointed time and L'Oreal was in a shed in the field with a little 13.2hh pony to keep her company. We put the halter on and led her over to the trailer. She was a bit reluctant, but we soon had her half in and half out. So far so good – when suddenly, the halter rope broke and off she went galloping round the field. That tore it (literally). That was when we first found out that she was difficult to catch. She just belted around with her friend, the little pony. We herded them into the shed, but when we tried to catch L'Oreal, the pony would get in between us and kick like funno! Then we had to get the pony out and start again. Somehow, we managed it, and it was all hands on deck again to get the mare into the trailer. Well, we eventually loaded the mare and shut the ramp quickly. Her soon-to-be-ex-owner asked us in for a cup of tea while L'Oreal got used to the trailer, so we went inside.

Once there we sat down and then all hell broke loose. The trailer started rocking about and we thought the canvas roof was going to suffer if we didn't get going quickly. Ron said that he would ride in the back with the horse for a little way, to try and settle her down. Most horses settle with the motion of the trailer on the road, so off we went and when we stopped to check on Ron, he said he would ride with her all the way just to be on the safe side. Apparently, she went to sleep on him though he complained about the driving as Nancy's husband had never driven with livestock before, and going down hills (of which there were a lot) he constantly put his foot on and off the brake, so I guess it wasn't a smooth ride. But, we managed to get home and took my new horse straight down to Dave's place for the next part of her education. I am really glad that Ron came as it turned out; we would never have had that 'mission accomplished' moment without him. He has since said it was a bad omen with the halter breaking and that we should have left her there, but, again, hindsight is a wonderful thing.

Dave set about breaking-in L'Oreal with Ron's help and I think things went mostly according to plan. Soon after, I had a 2-year-old that I could ride, but that also needed a lot of teaching. I had never done anything like this before, but I was glad to be back in the saddle. I used to get up early and take her out for an hour before I went to work. I soon found out that she was a cantankerous mare.

I have never forgiven Mr Pearce (Dave) for a trick that he played on me, as I was a complete novice with a horse that

## L'OREAL

had just been broken in. I was out for one of my evening rides when I had finished work and we were walking up the main road towards Stibb Cross. All of a sudden Dave caught us up and passed us on his own horse, and L'Oreal virtually sat in the road. What I hadn't realised was that she had never seen another horse coming up beside her before and so it took her by surprise. (We all live and learn though, and so I filed that information away). Once L'Oreal got used to it, we rode side by side for a couple of miles and were coming around Brown's Lane, about a mile and a half from home. Dave suggested we cut across one of the fields so that we could cut the corner of the road off, assuring me it would be ok with the farmer as Dave worked for him. Poor little innocent Annie said, "Okay, no problem". We opened the gate from horseback, went through and Dave took off at a gallop across the field. L'Oreal went berserk and just started bucking worse than funno, and more like a rodeo horse doing handstands! I was just deciding whether I should bail-out or not when she finally listened to the aids that I was giving her and stopped. We continued across the field where Dave was waiting, laughing his head off, but I had the last laugh as he obviously knew what would happen with a youngster and had done it to see me fall off –

which I didn't (although I'm not quite sure how). To this day I have never forgotten that mean trick, but I rode back home beside Dave with my head held high! (Oh, boy was I learning all the time!) I was glad to be able to un-tack and leave L'Oreal in her stable that night. Ron had since converted our old coalhouse into a stable, which was at the front of the cottage now and not down the bottom of the garden any more.

I continued to persevere with my cantankerous mare, as I could do nothing else if I wanted to ride. The last straw came one Saturday morning. I went around the back lanes and then she suddenly decided she was not going on any further. She would turn and go back, but not go forward. We had a big *contretemps*, which I eventually won and on we went again. I intended to go down the main road by Flat Tops and then on to the Southcott turning and back home through the lanes that I could canter on. Part-way down the main road she threw another hissy fit, in front of a milk tanker, bucking and trying to rub me off in the hedge. I managed to sort her out and was jolly glad when the turning to Southcott appeared and I could leave the main road. Just as I turned down it, Ron appeared behind me in the car to see if I was okay as he knew she had been playing up recently. He said, "Oh, I needn't have bothered – she's going very well," to which I harrumphed. I told him what had happened and he said that he would follow me home. I went down the hill absolutely livid with the mare and when I got to the bottom, about two miles from home. I dug my heels in and gave her a smack with the crop and sent her off as fast as she could lick. I knew it would be okay as it was uphill. We got to the main road and I trotted fast towards her stable, which was about another quarter of a mile away. When we got home, I jumped off, shouting about how I would never ride that horse again! Poor Ron thought that she had bolted with me – and was worried 'til he caught me up and saw how mad I was!

    I actually did sit on the mare one more time as we came back from a Sunday lunchtime at the Clinton Arms, Frithelstock and I said I would go out once more with Dave and his son for a ride. I tacked her up and mounted as Dave and Steven came up the road. The minute we set off I could not do a thing with her and she was up all over the place. I said, "That is it!" and as it turns out, it was. Ron called me a

## L'OREAL

"Wussie" and said he would ride her. Bearing in mind that he does not ride horses, I think it must have been the Double Diamond talking, as I believe it was advertised to work wonders! So, we swapped. I went in with Mum and Dad to get the dinner ready as they were only going to ride for a short time. After a while we heard a kerfuffle in the road. It was a long way away but I knew it had to be Ron and L'Oreal. Apparently they stopped at Dave's place while he went in to get something. When he came out, she played her usual tricks and refused to go on. Ron gave her a smack with the crop (a lot harder than I could do) and she put in a great big buck and deposited Ron on top of a bank, which he proceeded to slip down on his bottom (in his Sunday best I may add) through all the mud and water! He saw red, got straight back on her, and she did the same thing again. Apparently, after that they then took her into some really boggy ground and lunged her around and around. When she came back she did not have enough wind to blow out a candle and I was invited to ride her again. No way. I decided to cut my losses as me and L'Oreal were never going to see eye to eye. I wanted to sell her so that I could buy another horse –

one that I could try out properly first. Ron helped me out again and said he would buy her off me and so L'Oreal went out to live in Ashwater with Ron's brother, Denzil. He had the Post Office stores at Ashwater and his wife's father had given them some ground and he kindly said that he would look after her for a while. Whilst out there and during a thunderstorm she must have been frightened as Denzil rang to say she had badly gashed her face. We dashed out there and indeed I think she must have caught it on corrugated iron. She had the most awful gash on her face, right down to the bone, which you could see. We called the vet who said that it would be touch and go depending on how bad the crack was in her nasal bone – if the air bubbled through we would lose her. We went out every night and bathed and tended to her and she was, in all fairness, a very good patient. When we were certain that she was on the road to recovery she was put in several acres with Denzil's bullocks, which are unfortunately a species of animal that I am petrified of.

We went up to see her one evening in the summer and had walked across one field as she was in the next one grazing quite happily with the other animals. I only had flip-flops on as it one of those rare occurrences – a nice, dry summer. For some reason best known to herself, L'Oreal got "taken with the wap" – as they would say in the west-country, and went galloping round the field stirring all the bullocks up into a frenzy, one of which was the size of a15.2hh horse, if he was an inch!

This was horror of horrors for me, and how is it that animals always know if you are afraid of them? She chased the bullocks around and they were like raging bulls from a bullring, and charged for us snorting and stamping. Oh my god! Ron, who was not in the slightest bit worried, told me to get behind him, but oh no – I was nearly hysterical and just ran for it. The cattle did another circuit of the field, while I broke the hundred yards Olympic record (in flip-flops), trying the reach the gate before they caught up with me. I dared not look round, but I could hear the bullocks charging right behind me, getting closer and closer. I got to the gate and threw myself over, landing in a heap on the other side.

Safe at last, I looked back and there was Ron standing in the middle of the field laughing his head off! The cattle had ignored him, and had indeed been making for me and were stamping and snorting on the other side of the gate. I was a complete wreck by that time and had to go up to the pub and have a brandy – something I don't normally drink – to steady my nerves. In fact I think I had two!

L'Oreal, by the way continued to live up to her reputation. She went on to break someone's foot, and once whilst out hunting, she jumped over a bank, into a garden and rampaged through the chicken runs complete with rider in tow. Eventually, we had her back and decided to breed from her as she was never going to make a safe riding horse. We bred four foals from L'Oreal before we sold her on. One chestnut, which my friend bought when he was a 7-year-old and who always lived with us, until we lost him at 29-years-old; one little dun that unfortunately had its mother's temperament no-one could do a thing with; a Better By Far colt who went to a good home; and a beautiful big mare sired by Louella Deisterhof, a lovely Hanoverian. She was a pleasure to handle and went on to make a nice show jumper.

# SEARCHING FOR MY NEXT STEEDS

As I no longer 'owned' L'Oreal, I was on the scout for another pony and heard by word of mouth that a local riding school in Westward Ho! had a 14.hh pony for sale for £90. Nikki, who came to work with me in the Payroll office at Toy Works, also had a great love of horses and she knew Victor who owned the stables, so we went down to see her. What a pretty pony. Very rich red brown bay and a Thoroughbred type that looked as though she had been raced. As I had 'sold' my first horse to Ron, he could not object to Melody (she had been called Lily the Pink, but I changed her name to Melody), and so Nikki rode her back from the stables in Westward Ho! to my little plot in Langtree village that I still paid 50p a week for. Unfortunately though, not long after, I lost this little plot and then had to look for another friendly farmer. I was very lucky to find Mr Duncan who had a big field about two miles away that he said I could use in the winter.

    I had been saving for quite a while and as I had managed to buy Melody for just £70, I was on the lookout for another horse so that Nikki and I could go out together. We used to get the *Western Morning News* and scan through the pages. In those days it was a broadsheet with usually a page and a half of horses for sale. I was looking for something about 15.hh, but as usual things never run to plan. A riding stable near Bovey Tracey at Haytor was advertising three horses for sale and as I always had a penchant for greys (after Freckles) we duly rang and said we would like to see the grey gelding that was advertised for sale. Unfortunately that one was sold, but they had a black 10-year-old mare that they thought would suit me. The horses were due to go to Exeter horse sales if they weren't sold through the paper and that was the day after we were going down there. Well, we had already booked the day off of work so decided we would go anyway.

Off we set and got there about 10am. I got out of the car and there was this black heavyweight mare tied up, looking very like a 'giddy-up-a-ding-dong' horse. (How wrong can you be?) I took one look and said to Nikki, "I am not interested in *that*!" With that, the lady who part-owned the school with her husband came over, and said that this is the black mare advertised would I like to ride her? Before I could open my mouth to say no, Nikki piped up, "Yes please" (for which I shall be eternally grateful). So, mumbling under my breath, I grudgingly put my riding boots and hat on and climbed aboard. I had been told to go to the main road, turn right and ride for a mile then I could go into some woods and ride through and come out back at the riding school. As the horse and I were coming up to the main road – oh my god – there were two bright yellow telephone cable-laying lorries with a compressor running and a big pipe running and vibrating down the side of the road. I thought to myself, "Oh, this is going to be good, get prepared for a tussle!"

especially with the mare having a new rider aboard that she could test out. To my utter amazement, the mare proceeded to ignore the whole affair like it wasn't there, and we strolled off down the road really 'walking out', which I love. I deduced from that, that she was 200% traffic proof, which is always something I look for first in a horse.

We got to the woods and had a canter through them and by the time we arrived back at the riding school I had really fallen in love with her. She rode so much differently to how she looked! I dismounted and then Major Sheldon appeared on the scene and it transpired that she was actually his horse and used in the school occasionally. The only trouble was that she did like to canter on the spot and leapt around a bit, and the pupils tended to pay more attention watching her than to their riding. The Major then said he would take her in the school and put her through her paces for me to show me what she could do. She performed in the ménage, dressage and jumping etc., but then the show seemed to come to an abrupt end (I found out why at a later date). Major Sheldon came out of the ménage and told me that if I didn't have her she was going to Exeter horse sales the next day, and proceeded to gallop off into the distance up to the tor behind the riding school. I told Mrs Sheldon that I would think about it over lunch and then ring her later in the day with my decision.

I decided to have her, as she was so good when I 'tried her'. She had two names, and plenty others later in the twenty years that I had her, but not always from me! She was known as Beautiful Artist, and was also registered with the BSJA as Beautiful III, a Grade C show jumper. Now I had my horse (and I paid for her on that day), how was I going to get her home? Luckily for me they said that someone would be coming up to North Devon in the near future and for an extra £40 they would deliver her for me. Ah yes – deliver her for me – one little problem; I hadn't told Ron! I decided to ask my friends Cathy and Ian if she could be liveried at Tadworthy with them until I had made arrangements for somewhere nearer home at Langtree, and also tell Ron. They of course agreed, so there I was in the same boat again; I had a horse that Ron knew nothing about, and to make matters more complicated, I now had a pony to ride at home (usually on a Sunday afternoon) *and* a horse soon to be in Northam.

My first priority was to find some ground where I could keep her in. The previous places I had used were now no longer available and so I asked our milkman who had some land two miles away from our cottage, under Langtree Week, that he didn't use. He very kindly said I could keep her there and I asked him not to mention it to Ron as I had not "given him the good news" yet! But I knew I had to break the news pretty quickly as winter was fast approaching and things were going to get difficult for me.

Nikki and I used to go riding in Northam, me on Beauty (that became her name for obvious reasons – her being black and having Beautiful in her name, which then became the 'Beauts', pronounced Boots) and Nikki on Ian's December. The Beauts stayed at Northam for a month and then Nikki agreed to ride her back to Langtree for me (she was used to riding back from that part of the world for me by now!) I still hadn't done the hard bit: telling Ron!

I used to go and see Beauts every morning to check that she was all right. I would wait for Ron to go to work and take a bucket of food down to the field for her, absolutely petrified that he would have forgotten something and he would meet me going down there and ask me what I was doing. It never happened, and she was there for about two weeks. The opening hunt meet was fast approaching and I thought that perhaps he would not be so mad if I told him that I had a new horse to go hunting on. As I've said before, I am not a great lover of hunting but anything for a quiet life!

Soon came the morning of the Opening Meet of the Stevenstone Hunt which was to be at Thornehill Head Moor, about a half an hour's ride away from Langtree, on the 2nd November 1975. I took Ron up a cup of tea in bed and said I had better go and get the horse to go hunting. (He knew I was going as I had been cleaning tack the night before). "Oh," he said, "are you taking Melody?" "No," I said, "Nikki is riding Melody, and I am taking my new horse." I got a strange look. "New horse? What is that?" "Oh I have this black mare and she is kept at Jeff's under Langtree Week." Of course, although he pretended not to be, he was interested and so off I set on foot to the field, and the first time he set eyes on the Beauts was when I brought her back and put her in the converted coalhouse. She was a magnificent looking horse and I tacked-up and waited for Nikki to come up the road to meet me (Melody was in a stable at Dave's), so that we could hack to the Meet together.

We had an uneventful ride up to the Meet. Diane, from my office at work had come out because she had been in on the 'goings on' and was dying to see both Nikki and myself at the hunt. Ron was there and everyone he knew was saying "Oh, that's a nice horse – what's your missus riding?" Poor Ron! His only reply was "I have no idea, I only saw the mare for the first time this morning". Of course they all thought that he was telling 'porkies', but in fact it was the truth. We stayed with the hounds for about an hour and then hacked home.

We decided that Melody was probably a bit small and so I advertised her and sold her to someone that Ron knew and she ended up hunting on Exmoor, which was great for her as she could fly and really loved the wide-open spaces.

# OYSTER (AND THE TRAILER)

Now to get another horse! I was on a roll. Nikki and I saw an advert in the *Horse & Hound* for a 15.hh horse for sale at a posh stables in Minehead, so we had a day's holiday from work and went to see her. Her name was Oyster, and she was a lovely dapple grey Arabian mare. As Nikki was going to be riding her, she tried her out. She was another lovely mare, and so I bought her, and then had to find another piece of ground that I could keep her on. Luckily I found another very nice man, an uncle of Dave's wife and only 50 yards from where Beauts was kept and so Nikki and I now had two horses to go riding on and take to some local Riding Club shows. We had some fun and eventually I sold Oyster to some people in Barnstaple who later bought our trailer.

That reminds me of the stories attached to buying and selling our trailer – and so I will digress a little. Having bought the horses I needed a trailer to take us to shows. Actually, first I needed a vehicle with a tow hitch and enough power to pull a trailer with two horses in. We had a

## OYSTER (AND THE TRAILER)

Hillman Hunter with no hitch at the time and so I scoured the papers for something suitable. The very thing I needed was advertised: a Vauxhall Ventora, gold, with a vinyl roof, a 3.3 litre engine, and, the crowning glory, a tow hitch – all for £575 (it was 1975 after all). I went to see it and liked the look of it and the garage said that they would take our Hunter in part exchange, so I bought it. No need to test drive, I thought, as it had everything I wanted even down to black leather seats. I pulled out of the garage, stopped at the traffic lights and thought "Oh, the engine has stopped!" and I tried to start it again – you can imagine the awful noise that it made – because, no it hadn't stopped, it was just such a lovely quiet engine. Ron was delighted with the car and so now I had to go and purchase a trailer. I would never normally contemplate pulling a trailer with a car and had obviously never attempted it before, but I was eager to get back into the world of horses again, and that meant another scour of the equine pages in the *Western Morning News*. I saw one that I thought I could afford, but the unfortunate thing was that it was at Henry Bowers, a trailer agent in Chard. Oh well, nothing for it...

Another day off work, (good job there were three of us in the Payroll office in those days before computerisation came in and the office was diminished to two people) and with Diane manning the office we set off in the new car to Chard. We stopped on the way and had a Chinese meal in Honiton and then got to Henry Bowers. The trailer was lovely: wooden but not heavy, and it was duly hitched to the car. I never gave it another thought. The only thing that was peculiar was that every time I glanced in the rear view mirror, all I could see was trailer, and I had to get used to using the wing mirrors instead. I was quite proud of myself especially driving back through the middle of Exeter and we got home

## Estonia and Equines

without a hitch (well, not literally). Of course, driving a trailer without horses in it is so much easier than with horses in, so I wasn't really as clever as I thought I was. I couldn't reverse it very well either but my idea was that Ron would take us around as he now had a 'new toy' to play with.

Our first few forays went very well with Beauts and Oyster, and Ron took us to some Holsworthy Riding Club shows and indoor show jumping at Cholwell in Lifton. The crunch came when in May he took us to 'Larks and Sparks', which was a small Hunter Trials in Black Torrington. We had quite a good day out and loaded the horses to come home. Unfortunately, we took a wrong turning out of the estate and had to go up a steep hill to get back on the right road home. We got nearly to the top of the hill and – horror of horrors – we got stuck. The horses were standing back on the trailer ramp because of the incline and were raising the back of the car off the ground, and of course, as it was a rear wheel drive car there we were – stuck! Ron could not take his foot off of the brake as the handbrake alone would not hold the load. Nikki and I scrambled out quickly and stacked the heaviest stones and boulders that we could find against the rear wheels to stop the whole lot rolling back down the hill. We could not unload the horses, as they would have fallen out as soon as we let the ramp down. Nikki and I belted off to try and find a tractor or some other such vehicle that could tow the whole caboodle up over the brow of the hill. It was a long way back to the showground and at last we found someone who could help.

We staggered back up the hill and when we got there the road was empty. Mr Barker, who incidentally had brought Oyster over to us from Minehead, had seen the predicament that Ron was in as he was going into the ground through another entrance. He dropped his trailer and came back in the Land Rover and pulled it all up and over the hill without a lot of bother. That was when Ron decided that he did not think it was safe to take us and the horses out using this mode of transport anymore, and so our new mode of transportation then became Mr Barker, who was the most perfect gentleman. He always wore a cravat, a cap and had a pipe in his mouth. He was a very well educated man who had been – we found out later – part of the 633 Bomber Squadron. The trailer then went up for sale and so was bought by the very nice people in Barnstaple who had bought Oyster. We discovered that she had unfortunately developed laminitis but they had her insured for loss of use and then bred from her, so all was well.

# CASHELS GRACE AND NAUGHTY BEAUTS

In between selling Oyster and the trailer, I bought another horse called Cashels Grace. Nikki had given up riding by then and so I asked another friend – the Landlady of the local pub, the Clinton Arms, called Doris. (I used to work there on a Friday night after work, play for the ladies darts team and also stayed there when Ron was away working on long jobs) – to come down with me to Peter Tavy, to see a little 15.hh Thoroughbred mare. The mare was very small but with a very big heart and had bred two good foals, one of which was called Pomeroy, ridden by Rodney Powell and did well at Badminton. She was also a sibling of a good west-country racehorse, so Ron was quite happy when I intimated that I thought another purchase was in the offing. The seller, Mrs Lane delivered Grace to us herself and I found out afterwards that she had been going to sell her before but when she had inspected the stables she had promptly taken her back home again. I'm glad our establishment obviously passed muster.

I bought Grace in 1976 and by now we were looking for somewhere with some land to keep both our horses on, as it was getting increasingly difficult living in our end terrace cottage and depending on kind farmers to allow me to keep various horses on their land, and having the horses in different places made life difficult for us. In 1977 we bought West End Villa at auction on behalf of Ron's sister and brother-in-law. They lived in Hong Kong and were looking to have a base to come home to in Devon. It was very nerve-wracking for me as everything was sold in different lots and it was my one and only foray into an auction room. Ron loved it. We bought the house first, but of course then we needed some land to go with it. We managed to buy two lots and so we now had a big house and several acres, which amounted to four big fields. Ron was to renovate the house and in return, we could live there and have land to keep our horses on. The auction was completed in October 1977 and, as the house had not been lived in for about thirty years, Ron was working hard every night, after a hard day at work, up at the house. The garden and orchard were completely overgrown with brambles up to tree height and after he had put that to rights he renovated and decorated the whole house so that Beryl and Dave would have a bedroom and sitting room upstairs for when they came home to visit. At this time, Grace was kept in our converted coalhouse and Beauts lived out.

We had a telephone call the day after Boxing day from Mr Sarjeant who had the field next to Beaut's under Langtree Week, to say that she had somehow broken into his field and could we come and remove her and put her back into the proper field. We were very apologetic and went down to see where she had got through. We could not see anywhere that she had broken through, but on tracking her hoof prints it looked very much like she had jumped the fence, which had barbed wire and was about four feet and six inches high. After going back home to fetch the required building materials, we returned, armed with squared fencing wire, and Ron proceeded to erect a six foot high fence that should have kept even deer out. We then caught Beauty, who was very amenable, and took her back to her own field. Once in the field, though, things took a turn for the worse and she was not too happy at being brought back. I think the grass must have been greener on the other side! She started cantering around eyeing-up the steeply-sided field opposite. Ron and I walked along the path that she had made previously to where she had jumped out, to see what was about to occur because something obviously was. She lined herself up, and we were about ten yards from where Ron had erected the fence, quietly confident that all would be well. With that, the Beauts trotted passed us with her head in the air up to the fence. Ron ran in front of her waving his arms in the air yelling "Get back you Black Bugger!" Of course Beauts took no notice and popped over the high fence, showing us a clean pair of heels, literally.

I would not have believed it if I had not seen it myself. Oh dear. Back we went into Mr Sarjeant's field but no way was the mare going to be caught again and taken away from her fresh grass. I sheepishly went to Mr Sarjeant's house and apologised profusely and told him what had happened. He very kindly said "Not to worry", and that I could try to catch her the next day. A very cross Ron then went and made the fence a lot higher, still grumbling that it would not have to be that high to keep a whole herd of red deer out, and luckily it had the desired effect, because after being caught and put back, Beauts went and had a look at the fence the next day, but decided that now it probably *was* beyond her capabilities!

She was so naughty that we moved her up to West End Villa while Ron was renovating so that he could see her from our kitchen window in the cottage and keep an eye on her. I looked out one morning and guess what? Beauts was not where she was supposed to be, but was in the next field. Off we went again to see where she had got out. We found a place in the hedge that was lower than the others and so piled up a lot of logs etc so that piece was as high as the remainder of the hedge, and put Beauts back in the field that she should have been in. The next morning, I looked out of the window and there she was on the other side again! After work Ron went up and piled things even higher. The next morning, same again, she had escaped. The following day was Saturday and I went up with Ron and he filled the gap even more. I had already put her in her correct field and she watched Ron working. When he had finished saying, "Ha! I've got her now," she did one circuit of the field and charged flat out at the place where the gap had been and sailed over under our noses. I swear that horse knew what we were thinking!

Finally, Ron got the place filled high and wide and once again she gave up her escapology. She then went through a phase of being very difficult to catch, and Val had to bring another horse out of the field for her to follow while I hid in the hedge then shut the gate behind her, which meant that she was trapped in a lane. Once she knew she was trapped she just stood there as if to say, "What is all the fuss about?"

# IVOR

I have a good friend called Ivor, who was an international show jumper, and when he gave that up he was an amateur jump jockey for a while. We had some good times together while he was living with one of our other good friends who is a Baroness. Although she never used the title, she spoke like a Baroness, but swore like a trooper! She was a very popular landlady of a local west-country pub.

Ron and I often went over to the pub in the week and used to go racing and to point-to-points with them. One of our trips turned out to be very eventful. It was a trip to Towcester racecourse. We set off in the lorry on a Thursday: Mary, Ivor (who was driving the lorry) Ron, myself and Mike (who was the local blacksmith and decided to come along for the ride and a 'jolly'). In the back were the horses: Arne Folly, Ivor's mount, who was racing the next day and Tiny Titmouse, a lovely, little old pony who was companion to any horse that had to go away anywhere. We had booked to stay B&B at the Brave Old Oak in Watling Street, Towcester, a lovely looking old-fashioned pub with a four-poster in one room. We arrived at the racecourse at about 6 o'clock, and that's when things started to go wrong! The gates were shut so we could not get in and unload 'Arthur J' as Ivor's horse had come to be known, and Tiny Titmouse. Ron, being athletic in those days said, '"No problem!" and proceeded to jump the iron fence at the side. Unfortunately, it was an old fashioned one with posts that looked like spears, and yes, you've guessed it, he put his hand on top of one as he vaulted and the pointed spear when straight through his hand. There was no blood but a hole at the base of his finger with chords (sinews) sticking out. We found out it was chords as Ron thought it was straw or some such thing sticking to his hand, but when he tried to pull it off his finger moved! Nonetheless, he managed to unlock the gates from the inside and we unloaded our charges and bedded them down for the evening before walking back to the pub and checking-in. Ron and I 'baggsied' the four-poster (well, I had done the homework and the booking so I got the spoils).

After we had settled in we went down to the bar for a drink and decided to book a table there for our evening meal. We were half way through our main meal when the manager came to us and said there was an urgent phone call for Mary (her son was 'minding' the pub for the 2 days that we were going to be away). Mary came back ashen faced. The pub was badly on fire and so she obviously wanted to leave straight away to go back. We ordered her a taxi and so she set off back to Devon at 8.00pm leaving us with the horses. We finished our meal and then for some reason Ivor ordered a bottle of champagne and we went to Mike's room and sat there contemplating what was going to happen in the morning as the owner (Mary) had gone home, and Ron, Mike and myself did not know the protocol – and Ivor just did the riding! We sat talking quietly and at about 11 o'clock the phone rang. I answered it and was asked if we could keep the noise down as the man in the next room was trying to get to sleep! We were all rather nonplussed at this request as we were not doing anything other than talking, but we all dispersed and went to our respective rooms.

We were all up at 5am next morning, because we wanted to go and walk the course, as Ivor had not ridden around it before. It was a lovely morning, but we still had no news from Mary – there were no mobiles then – but the walk around Towcester racecourse was beautiful. We went and checked on Arthur J and Tiny Titmouse and they were fine. We then walked back to the pub for breakfast and to see if we could catch up with news on the pub fire. While we were having breakfast the person who served it to us said that they had had ructions that morning as someone had had an early morning call at 5.30 am and he hadn't ordered it! He was quite irate as he couldn't get back to sleep again. I thought we were all innocent but after breakfast Mike confessed that he had done it in response to the phone call the previous night! Jolly well served him right as far as I was concerned.

We spoke to Mary that morning, and she told us that half of the pub had been gutted, but she was glad that she had gone back the previous night. Our next problem was the bandaging and tacking-up of Arthur J before the race, as this was usually Mary's domain. David Barons, a local west-country trainer that we knew had horses running, seemed like a good person to ask, so we decided that we would seek out his Head Boy and see if he would mind bandaging Arthur J for us. He said that it was fine and that because our race was not until late in the afternoon it should all work out fine.

At lunchtime, we went into the pub across the road from the racecourse for a meal and Barons' Head Boy was in there (I use the term Head Boy loosely, as he was a fairly ancient Irish man). We bought him a couple of glasses of Guinness for his trouble and he said that he would meet us in the tacking-up area. The time duly came but he was nowhere to be seen. Ron and I did the best we could with the tacking-up (with Ivor's help), and then we found a groom to do the bandaging. Off they all set. After all that, the tack was okay, but the bandages came undone after one circuit and so Ivor had to pull-up Arthur J. We packed everything up and loaded up the horses and started our weary way home with poor Ivor driving the lorry back to Devon. On the way back, who did we see broken down on the motorway with a flat tyre but David Baron's turn-out! We arrived home without further incident. Ron and Mike in the back with the horses and me trying to keep Ivor awake, talking about old show jumpers, both people and horses!

We had another 'incident' with Ivor, which, in a roundabout way, involved horses. In February 1977 Mary decided that she was going on holiday abroad with Ivor – she also decided that it would be great if Ron and I could go as well. Well, as drink was probably in and wit was out, we said "What a great idea!" As I had been to Majorca in 1967 it was decided that I would do the research and booking. I did not mind as I got to choose the airline (knowing my fear of flying I was only going to fly with a reputable company and that, as far as I was concerned in those days, was British Airways, and so I chose a holiday from their own brochure). We were going for a week at the end of February to Puerto Pollensa and staying in the Illa D'Or. We were flying early in the morning and so we set off around midnight. We got to Heathrow around 4.30am and found a car park and parked the car (Ivor's white Capri – we had listened to The Shadows all the way up to the airport!) I was getting decidedly jittery, so when we went to a breakfast bar, all I could manage was a glass of orange juice. We went through the magnetic archway and then got stopped and asked how much money we had with us – that was in the day when you could not take more that £50 out of the country. Ron had £32 on him and so we were allowed through. I did not know that in fact he had stuffed some more money into his socks in case of emergency! If I had, I would have looked very guilty, so it was just as well that I didn't. That might not sound like much money, but bear in mind the holiday cost £99 per person for half board in a four star hotel, flying scheduled British Airways Tristar! I know, unbelievable.

When we were asked to board, I was thinking about backing out and so Ron, Ivor and Mary pushed me in front to make sure that I got on the plane. It was a beautiful flying day and after a couple of medicinal brandies, I felt decidedly better. We arrived in lovely sunshine and then had an hour and a quarter trip to our hotel. It was beautiful, and right by the sea. There were lovely soft leather armchairs and sofas in the lounge bar that just went 'pouffe' and folded around you as you sat in them, and the food was brilliant. We had only booked half board and I wished that we had booked full-board as it was only another £1 per day if we had booked in England. Anyhow most days we went back for lunch and it was because of this that the aforementioned 'incident' occurred.

We had arrived on the Wednesday, and on the Saturday, Arthur J had been entered for a race at Plumpton. Obviously, Ivor, who had been going to ride him, could not, and so a good local jockey called Paul had been substituted. Anyhow, we went out for a drive after breakfast in the hire-car (I forgot to say that within the £99 for the holiday a hire car was also included). We came back to the harbour at lunchtime and found a tapas bar and went in for a couple of drinks. The 'landlady' or whatever they are called in Majorca turned out to be English, so Ivor and Ron were well away. After a couple of drinks Mary and I decided that we would like lunch back at the Illa D'Or. Ron and Ivor declined and so we left them there. What a *mistaka to maka!* After our lovely lunch, we strolled back to the tapas bar to find Ron anxiously walking about outside looking for us. "What's happened?" we asked. "Oh boy, am I glad to see you," said Ron. "Where's Ivor?" we asked, and to that question Ron pointed and all we could see were Ivor's feet sticking out from behind some dustbins. Oh boy, was Mary mad.

It turn out that Ivor had rung England – not once but twice! Once to see how Arthur J had performed (which turned out to be not very well as Paul had 'dismounted' at the first fence!) and secondly, to speak to his two boys who were at home. Consequently, he had run up a big bill on the telephone and over the bar! He had gone a bit mad on the Spanish gin and so, disappeared to the 'loo'. Ron thought he had been a long time and went in to fish him out. He had slumped down behind the door and they had a heck of a job to get him out. Ron got him outside and put him on a chair and told him to stay there until he had sorted things out with the owners of the bar. Next time he looked, Ivor was staggering along veering from side to side nearly falling into the harbour. As luck would have it he staggered to the wall behind the dustbins and collapsed in a heap behind them, thus only his feet poking out when we arrived on the scene! He had run up such a big bill that Mary and I had to go back to the hotel (at a faster pace this time) to collect some traveller's cheques and change some in the hotel, so that we could go back and pay Ivor's bill.

Mary was like Queen Victoria – 'Not Amused' – as the bar and phone bill was nearly £30 and that was their spending money 'up the creek' so to speak. Ivor had also been the one that was nominated to drive as he had driven abroad a lot of times before when he was show jumping. Now we had a problem as he was *non compos mentis* behind the dustbins – still it could have been worse: he could have been 'in the drink,' so to speak! Well, nothing for it, Ron would have to drive! Luckily it was only a short way back to the hotel. Ron hoisted Ivor out from the dustbins and put Ivor's arm round his neck. Now Ivor's feet were not touching the ground – Ron being 6 feet tall and Ivor, a small jockey, of just over 5 feet. We 'poured' him into the car and I sat in the back with him on the short drive back to the hotel. If you have ever seen a cartoon where, for example, Donald Duck has been hit on the head and his eyes were going round… well, I think you will get the picture: a closer facsimile I have never seen. Oh, I forgot to mention, he was also a horrible green colour. Arriving back at the hotel safely, there was no way we were going to get him out of the car and so we left him in there to sober up, checking on him every so often. He finally surfaced at around 8 o'clock at night and managed to get to his room. Ron took him up a cup of coffee, (Mary was still not speaking to him) then the three of us went in the dining room for dinner. The Spanish waiter said, "Only three for dinner tonight? Ah, the Spanish gin is very strong." I am afraid that Ivor has never lived that day down.

The rest of the holiday was fabulous and without incident until it came to flying home. We all piled into the bus to go to the airport and then the bus engine just died.

After several abortive attempts to start the engine we all had to pile out again and the decision was made to send for another bus. While we were waiting, the driver rallied round some people to see if the bus could be 'bump started'. Just as the second bus pulled into the hotel, the engine of our original bus leapt into life and we piled back on again (well, it saved moving all the luggage around). Our only problem now was that the flight we were on was a scheduled flight and not a charter, so there was no way that it was going to wait for a late bus. I have never had such a hair-raising ride in a bus, and we bounced all over the road trying to make the airport on time. We screeched to a halt outside, got out, and were virtually waved straight through. We just had to pass through security. Ivor, of course, got taken away for a thorough search, as he unfortunately was wearing thick twill trousers with a very wide seam, and they seemed to be worried that he was trying to smuggle something in them. We just made it on to the plane and thankfully had an uneventful flight back to Heathrow. As I was scared of flying, everyone gave me their prawn cocktail – trying to make me feel better – as it was my favourite food and airline food was of a better calibre in those days. We landed and made it back to the car, and were soon off speeding back down the motorway with Captain H. "Flying at 80 miles an hour at ground level," as he kept on telling us. As it happened, we had been very lucky as we found out later that a spring had gone in the rear of the car and anything could have happened at that speed, but we made it home safely.

Another equine story involving Ivor was the time that we went to Aintree. It had always been Ivor's dream to jump Beecher's Brook and so we had gone to Ascot sales the previous autumn to see if we could purchase a horse exactly for the job. Mary, Ivor, Ron, Mary's son, Shaun, and myself all went up in our Ventora to the sales. We stayed overnight at the Cricketers' Arms in Ascot and went to the sales next morning. Ivor found the horse that he fancied that had qualified to run in the Topham Trophy at the The Grand National Meeting. He was called Hariscan. So it was that in April 1977 Mary, Ivor, Ron and myself were all crammed in the front of the cab of the horsebox together with our springer spaniel, Mitch, beetling up the M5 and M6 to Liverpool. Again, it had been down to me to sort out the accommodation and so I booked the Liverpool Crest Motel, which was fairly close to the racecourse. Ivor was going to ride in the Topham Trophy on the Friday afternoon.

As the lorry was our only means of transport we had left it in the car park after depositing Hariscan, and of course his travelling companion, Tiny Titmouse, in their accommodation at the racecourse, and we had left Mitch to sleep in the lorry as well. That turned out to be quite a good idea, as we found out in the morning. We had a meal in the Motel and retired to bed early, as we were going to have a fairly early start in the morning. A salesman that we had been having a drink with the previous evening was in reception as we came down for our breakfast trying to find out where his car had disappeared to, from said car park. The police were called and the car was found a mile down the road, minus all its wheels. We dashed out to check the lorry, but thankfully it was intact. Clearly, Mitch had done a good job.

After all the excitement in the morning, it turned out to be a great day. We had lunch with all the famous jump jockeys and then came the time for Ivor to get ready for his race. Fortunately, unlike our previous escapade, luckily this time there had been no fiery mishaps and Mary was there to tack-up and bandage Hariscan. Ron led Hariscan into the parade ring pre-race and was spotted on the television by quite a few friends, even though we had not told anyone that we were going up there. It was quite amusing really as Shaun had recorded the whole thing and Richard Pitman had described Ivor as Mary's son! Mary was 'Queen Victoria' again, and it was another thing that Ivor never lived down. It just showed that Richard Pitman had not done his homework properly. Ron was determined to get on the racecourse somehow. He would not have stood a chance in this day and age, but back then he charged on to the course and went down by the jump called 'The Chair' and just shouted 'Press' just for some attention!

    We knew Beecher's Brook was a really big jump as when we arrived on Wednesday evening, we had all four of us (plus Mitch) walked the course. I had platform boots on! It was 1977 and I was stupid enough not to have thought to pack any Wellington boots, but there was no way I was going to Aintree and not walk the course. The jumps that stood out in my mind were the obvious ones. The Chair – Ron stood in the ditch on the take-off side and could not touch the jump and the ground at the front of the ditch at the same time. The ditch also had a gate at the end to let the horses out if they had refused. Beecher's Brook – what an awful jump... all I can say is that I am glad that all the jumps have been altered now. Ivor stood on Ron's shoulders and he could not see over the top of the jump and it was also on the turn on sidling ground. *Very* awkward for the horse, and a lot used to fall there in earlier years. 'Valentines' was also a huge jump with a right hand turn after it. Mitch tried to jump every jump on the course and thoroughly enjoyed himself, and I must be the only person to have walked around Aintree in platform boots,

## Estonia and Equines

not once but twice as I did it again early Thursday morning!

Alas, Hariscan turned out to be 'Haris-can't'. Ivor and his steed jumped the first three jumps but then got brought down by a horse tracking him at the fence before Beecher's Brook, so poor Ivor never fulfilled his dream to jump Beecher's. Ivor needed to be brought back by ambulance and someone caught Hariscan and led him back towards the enclosure. Ron went running down the track to meet the horse and led him back to us. Poor Hariscan had two horseshoe-shaped marks on his rump where the horse behind had caught him. We all went back to the jockeys' area had some tea and then loaded up Hariscan and Titmouse and began wending our weary way home. We finally got back to Ashwater at 3.30am and home at 4.00am. I had to be at work next morning at 8.00am to count cash and put wages in envelopes, as it was done in those days – no BACS then! I got there, but it seemed a long day!

When I bought my horse the Beauts, she would not jump at all – two refusals at the first jump and a refusal at the second – that was the norm when I first started jumping her and very often came out of the ring feeling a bit of a 'Wally'. I soon found out that one thing you could not do was hit Beauty behind the saddle with the crop. She would take a tap down the shoulder and respond but behind the saddle would make her stop dead and she would *not* move at any cost.

I was not a 'showing' person, and my friend wanted to show her in a working hunter class. No problem. They went round and round and round the ring, as they were asked to, and as they were being called into line, Beauts having had a smack, showed her annoyance and stopped dead. My friend tried everything she could but to no avail and looked panicky at me outside the ring and mouthed to me, "What shall I do?" "Get off quick!" I mouthed back. She did, and luckily with that change the Beauts allowed herself to be walked into the line-up. Of course my friend and I were both dreading what was going to happen when the judge got on to ride her. The Beauts, being true to her nature, was just the opposite of what was expected. The judge – a man and not what Beuts was used to – got on while we waited with baited breath. Off she moved and went perfectly for him like butter would not melt in her mouth, and she finished in the rosettes, though needless to say that was the end of her being entered for a show class! My nerves couldn't stand it!

The Beauts and Ivor never got on very well either. Ivor decided he wanted to jump at Holsworthy Agricultural Show and as Beauts was a registered grade BSJA show jumper we entered her for that class. He was in the practice arena and unfortunately did the unthinkable – gave her a reminder behind the saddle (although I had told him that she would not take a reminder!) True to form she stopped on take off stride and catapulted Ivor straight into the wing of the practice jump! He was mad because he lost face, and so things deteriorated rapidly from then on and needless to say they got eliminated for refusals.

Not long after this I had unlocked the secret of getting her to jump rather than stop – well nearly – we still had the odd moment! I decided that I would like to go to a small show that was being held at Ashreigny. Ron and I went down to the field that the Beauts was in and loaded her up. So far, so good. We had just started off and there was an almighty clatter and the trailer started doing a dance. The Beauts had decided that she wanted to travel with her head out over the ramp! No problem! When we arrived at Ashreigny we parked our car and trailer and were sitting talking when lo and behold, who should we spy across the other side of the field but Ivor and Mary's horsebox. We went over to have a word with them and they had brought a friend with their pony, Araminta, and had also brought Shaun's old pony Atalanta for their friend's daughter to ride as well. Well, one thing led to another and before I knew it I was being challenged to a 'Chase-Me-Charlie'. For the uninitiated this is a gymkhana event whereby a single pole is jumped, starting on the ground and then raised by one or two holes on the wings of the jumps every round. As it is a gymkhana event it gets difficult for ponies and horses not used to doing it because when it gets a lot higher it has no 'ground-line'. The 'The Famous International Show Jumper' – Ivor – challenged me and the prize was £1 to the winner! He said that he would beat me no problem. Ron was looking after the jump and so when no one was using the practice jump we had our little competition. Much to Ivor's disgust, the Beauts and I beat him.

    I took her into the show jumping where she proceeded to jump a lovely round until we got to the last jump, at which point she stopped and there was no way that she was going to jump it, so Ivor had the last laugh on me. Then he decided that he wanted to go in for an actual gymkhana class on Atalanta, and so we entered the Parents' Race, which was The Gretna Green – this is where the 'passenger' stands at the other end of the ring and you start off on the whistle, gallop to them and they leap on behind you as you turn and then gallop back. Well, that's the theory anyway! Ours must have looked very funny because we were the oldest in it anyway, and I still don't know why I agreed to do it! Ivor said to me, "Don't worry, when you get to the end, just turn for home and kick-on! I will jump up, just keep going!" So I took him at his word. Atlanta, with me aboard, galloped down to the other end of the ring where Ivor was waiting (what I had not entered into the equation was the amount of alcohol that he had consumed – not that it was a lot – but it certainly had an effect on his 'leaping'). I duly turned Atalanta and kicked-on, as instructed. Ivor tried to leap and missed! He then grabbed hold of me and nearly pulled me off, but managed to get up behind me, by which time my riding hat had fallen down over my eyes. Everyone else had finished and had quite a laugh as we were weaving our way back to the finish, because I could not see where we were going and Ivor was clinging to me like a leech whilst I was trying to keep my balance! We were definitely too old for gymkhana-ing I thought! Still, it was another great show that I will never forget.

The 'Bag of Monkeys' called Beauts at
Cholwell Equestrian Centre near Launceston

Buckfastleigh point-to-point: Me, Ron and Michael in the mud and rain!

Buckfastleigh Point-to-Point: Michael and L'Oreal

Miss Gold, Ron, Me, Ivor and Mary at Exeter Races 1979

Lovely Loopy Lancer 1990

Splodge showing her potential 1991

The Two Ages of Splodge — with Didge
(top) and Charlie (above)

The Three Amigos aboard Mr 'P', Star
and 'B' (in that order) 2008

# GABRIEL, TAMAR, FLAUNTY & MISS GOLD

When we had just moved to West End Villa, Ron was offered a two-year-old sire by Collision Course, at a very cheap price. We went to see her and Ron decided to buy her. He started breaking her in and very soon we had another horse to ride. We took her to quite a few shows; my friend used to ride her while I rode Beauty. She did vey well, both indoor and outdoor, and then Ron decided that he would like her to race. She went up to a racing yard near Chulmleigh, and raced under Mary's name as owner, and of course Ivor rode her. Her first race was at the Devon and Exeter racecourse, and we all went up there to watch. She jumped the first hurdle brilliantly and we thought that we were on a roll. Not for the first time, I found out that you never count your chickens! At the second fence on the far side of the course, she suddenly disappeared from sight. Oh dear! She got up and continued, riderless. With bated breath we waited for the ambulance to collect Ivor and bring him back to the weighing room. He was none the worse for the fall, thank goodness, but his riding whip was full of grass and he wasn't too happy. He said that she was tracking the horse in front and just didn't see the hurdle and crashed straight through it without rising. We had a deflated trip back home. There endeth the first lesson!

Our next trip out was to Taunton, where Ivor had two rides: Slide Over Baby and Miss Gold. He came off Slide Over two hurdles from home and Ron and I rushed down to see if he was alright, as he was not moving. Just as we arrived, the ambulance overtook us and put him in the back, so we trekked back to the weighing room to see how he was. He was okay, but the doctor would not let him take his next ride and so we had to find another jockey. He was called George and although he took the ride, he had no intention of trying, especially on a novice horse. He pulled her up after one circuit although she jumped well. Her final outing was at Chepstow but neither Ron nor I could not make it. Of course, what happened? She came second and beat the favourite St Barbe! I did have a nice official photo of her and so I had it made into an oil painting as a Christmas present for Ron – so that memory has not got lost in the annals of time.

While at West End Villa we sent Beauty to stud as the general consensus was that she would breed a good foal. True to Beauts' form, she stayed at stud all summer and was then tested 'not in foal'. She even ran loose with the stallion. She lost so much weight that when Ivor and I went to fetch her we did not recognise her: she was in the stable waiting to be collected and we were running around the field trying to catch a black cobby looking horse that did not want to be caught. After seeing the slimline Beauts, I can see how we made that mistake!

While the Beauts was at stud, I bought Gabriel to ride and hopefully school-on during the summer and then sell for a profit at the end. I asked Dad if he wanted to come in with me and so he did. Gabriel came from Ermington and Val and I went down to see him. He was advertised as 15.3hh, 6-years-old and half Thoroughbred, half Cleveland Bay. What a lovely surprise when we eventually got there; he was at least 16.1hh, a nice looking horse and lovely to ride – so I said yes straight away. He was an absolute dream except for one thing: he was a wussie! I took him show jumping and coming out of the clear round jumping, the steward went to give him a handful of grass and Gabriel looked at her and took fright as if she were from another planet. I jumped him all summer and he was very easy to sell on, as a novice could ride him. I doubled mine and dad's money on him.

Next came Tamar, a 15.hh three-quarter Arab. He was 6-years-old and had never been shod in his life. We got him used to the blacksmith and took him to a few shows but he never really liked jumping and so I was lucky to sell him to a young girl from Ilfracombe who just wanted to get on something and gallop off – well, she could certainly do that on him! The legacy that he left us with was teeth marks in the vinyl roof of our car! I was holding him at a little local show when all of a sudden he took a chunk out of the roof. What a good job it was our car I was holding him by, as vinyl roofs were all the rage then and it could have been quite embarrassing, not to mention, expensive!

I then saw a 5-year-old horse called Flaunty, advertised down in South Devon, sired by Flandre II, out of a good racing mare – so Val and I went down to see her. She was about 15.2hh and a lovely dark dappled bay with a big white blaze but she had a 'wall eye' – which did detract from her beauty somewhat. She also had a very dipped back, which I always find comfortable. She was kept on a farm and the owner said that his daughter had been riding her. Val offered to try her out so that I could look at her properly, and so rode her round the field, but we knew that she was a bit 'green' and that is exactly what she looked like. It was a bit odd that the owner seemed to want to lead her all the time, but we did not think anything of it there and then. He led her back, hanging on to her the bridle, to the farm. We discussed the mare and thought that she would be quite a good buy for the summer and so we arranged for Mr Barker to bring her back in the trailer. Again, there were some peculiar antics from the owner as Mr Barker said that he ran alongside the trailer all the way to the end of the road, even though the mare had loaded very well.

It is funny how everything suddenly starts dropping into place... She was as good as gold to catch, in the stable and in traffic and to ride *the first time*. The second time, Val had come over to take her out on her own on a Saturday and I had gone up to the Green Dragon Pub in Langtree as Mum and Dad had come over for the day. I had not been up there for half and hour when the phone rang. It was Val saying that Flaunty had refused to go on, bucked her off and galloped home. Luckily, Flaunty knew where 'home' was, but even so it was along the main road! I was so mad, but I knew that the horse had to go out again straight away. I thought it best if I rode her this time, so asked Val to tack-up and ride Miss Gold instead. I went home and Flaunty out. She was very good with me that afternoon. However, it was a case of 'The Girl with the Curl in the Middle of her Forehead' syndrome – as I was soon to find out.

I rode her every weekend and also another friend came and exercised her as well twice a week. For most of the time she behaved herself but things would always come out of the blue. We were cantering up a lane and she was going perfectly when from nowhere she put in a rodeo show: real handstands. Just when I was thinking that I was about to hit the deck, I managed to pull her together and she stopped and went on like butter would not melt in her mouth. She went perfectly for my friend Anita in the week (Anita used to jump BSJA and point-to-point) when she came out of the gate and went up the main road, but there, again, she exploded out of the blue. Anita didn't want to ride her anymore and then my blacksmith, who also point-to-pointed, said he would ride her. He jumped on in the yard and he didn't even get out of the gate. She put her show on in the yard just like a bucking bronco. I took her indoor jumping at Cholwell. We were actually going to a show somewhere else but it was cancelled so we 'rocked-up' to the indoor school and asked if we could hire it. Again, butter would not melt in her mouth and she jumped quite well. The next day I had a phone call from her previous owner asking how she was going. All was becoming clear. When I told him that I had taken her indoor jumping he was most surprised, and then it came out; he said that he had to ring and find out how she was going as she had bucked his daughter off in the road and come home and they had never ridden her again. There was no way I was going to tell him how she had been behaving, but how silly are people not telling the truth when selling a horse – it could have caused a really serious accident.

An acquaintance of ours wanted to go to the hunt Opening Meet and asked if we had a horse she could borrow. The only one spare was Flaunty, and I told her exactly what the horse was like, but said she was welcome to borrow her if she wanted to. They came up and boxed her to their farm, took her hunting, and when they brought her back they obviously thought I was a complete nutcase because she had behaved herself perfectly. What a Jekyll and Hyde personality! She was a horse that I was never going to get to the bottom of and so I decided to take her to Wadebridge market and sell her. I had never done that before and didn't really want to do it then, but I did not see any other way.

Mr Barker arrived in the morning and off we set. Everything was going to plan until we were just coming into Holsworthy, and there was an almighty rumpus in the back of the trailer (good job it was Mr Barker's sturdy old Beaufort). He looked in his side mirror and he could see Flaunty's leg sticking out of the jockey's door. He stopped immediately (luckily there was a lay-by right there) and both me and Val got out and took down the ramp. She had got her foot stuck in the hay net, struggled, and gone down. All things considered she was very good and did not struggle. We undid the net and we also did not have the partition in the trailer, so she managed to get up. Well, there was no way that we could continue now so we decided to walk her the mile down the road to a farm that belonged to the chairperson of the Holsworthy Riding Club. She was very accommodating and kept her overnight and then Mr Barker brought her back home the next day.

What to do now? As luck would have it, Anita rang me and said that she knew someone who would like her. She had told them all about her and would you believe it, they came up, rode her, (she was on her best behaviour) had her vetted and bought her. I breathed a big sigh of relief as I thought I would have to keep her as a brood mare.

# MOVING HOUSE (AND STABLES)

In 1982 we moved from West End Villa – although we had lovely stables that Ron had built there, I always hated it because the main tourist traffic route went through the village and I was always afraid that people would leave gates open and the horses would get out or the cats would get run over. In fact, both things happened. We had two cats called Starsky and Hutch. Hutch was a lovely cat, who absolutely adored Mars Bars, and when I sat down would curl himself around my neck like a scarf. I got back from hacking one Sunday afternoon to be told that he had been killed on the main road. Luckily, Ron had already buried him but it broke my heart. The other thing that happened was that walkers came up our lane and left three gates open. Whether it had been done on purpose or not, I do not know, but five horses were out on the main road. Luckily, we had good neighbours who had rounded them up and put them in one field – all except one: yes, you've guessed it, The Beauts. She was happily grazing on someone's lawn up the road. Of course, it had to belong

## MOVING HOUSE (AND STABLES)

to the 'poshest' house in the village, where a captain from the Navy lived. I apologised profusely and cringed when I saw the whacking great hoof prints in the lawn and told them that they would soon disappear. Ron offered to come up and repair the lawn, but they were very gracious and said not to worry and were glad that I had caught my horse and that she was uninjured.

So, I was very happy when we moved further into the country about three and a half miles away and were no longer on a main road; the only thing that passed our cottage was the milk lorry, which in those days carried milk churns.

We had bought a 'two-up, two-down' cottage with six acres of land. But our problem was that we were now downsizing from twenty-two acres and we had eleven horses! Ron went up even before the completion was through and built his workshop and pulled down the two wooden stables. We moved in April 1982 just as the Falkland War started. We did all the removals ourselves, with Ron taking over tractor-loads of furniture, time after time. It was a good job that the weather was fine. I remember taking the last load with the dogs and cats in Ron's work van, which was also filled to the gunwales with TVs and mattresses, etc. That just left the horses.

We had asked around the area that we were moving to as to whether there was any available ground to rent as obviously six acres was not going to be enough (the general rule of thumb is one acre per horse). We were very lucky and found some land about six miles away for the youngsters. The only trouble was you had to walk down through a big field, and then through some woods to get there. Well, beggars can't be choosers, and so we just had to put up with it and be thankful that we had found somewhere. Then came the fateful day of 'moving of the livestock.' Luckily, we had dear Mr Barker to help as well as Ron, Dave and my friend Val. We took the young stock, two by two, to our rented ground (this was fairly easy as Ron had made a corral and they could be herded into the trailer). We then took the riding horses to our new field at home (Beauty, Grace and Miss Gold) and L'Oreal went to stud. All went well. Then Ron had to start building stables before the winter set in. He concreted the base and set the shell up in wood (we had decided to have wooden stables as they are much warmer than breeze block as our stables at West End Villa were). There was many a time that Val and I had Grace and Beauty tied up to the wooden frame before hacking or going to a show, but by the winter we had some beautiful stables, and we had managed to sell all of the young stock, except for L'Oreal's first chestnut foal which we had decided to keep, and called him Laddie (his registered name was West End Lad).

Ron broke him in and I used to come home from work and ride him in the evening, but after a long day at work this became quite tiring and so we decided to sell Miss Gold as Val said she would like to ride Laddie.

We had sold some of the young stock to people associated with the local riding stable and Maria (the daughter there) had been up to our stables several times. She had asked to have first refusal if Miss Gold ever came up for sale. I contacted her and said she was welcome to come up and ride her, and if she wanted to go out with somebody (namely her father who owned their stables) that was no problem as they could ride The Beauts too. The riding stable owner had told us that he used to ride in the army, and point-to-point. They came up and off they went over to the moor about half a mile down the road, which in those days was not

## MOVING HOUSE (AND STABLES)

fenced off. My only instruction to 'an upstanding man who owned a riding stable and point-to-pointed' was whatever you do, don't put the Beauts' feet on grass as she would just started leaping and bouncing and jumping all over the place. I found from the wife of her previous owner that that was the reason the stables in Haytor sold her – because all the riding students were busy watching Beauty's antics rather than concentrating on what they should be doing! Though I have to add that she was safe as the Bank of England to ride – although she didn't look it – and I never came off her in all the time that I rode and jumped her. The few times I could have come off, she somehow or other saved me.

You should have seen Maria and her father's faces when they eventually arrived back. Maria was laughing her head off. Her father who was white as a sheet, bounced into the yard – or rather Beauts did. He jumped off, threw the reins at me and said, "I really do not know how you could ride that!" with some venom and stormed off. Maria said that on the way back he had gone onto the moor with Beauty and of course she had gone into 'Beauty mode' which, once started, could not be stopped and also once started she pulled like a train. I suppose he thought that she was not going to stop and was about to tank off with him. Well, I – like Maria – thought it was hilarious and she bought Miss Gold anyway. I did hear that her father had tried to point-to-point her and had fallen off, which I fully understood. I don't think that he was as good as he thought he was!

Not long after that they had a fire down at the stables which we heard about on the local radio at about 6am, and of course rushed down to see if we could help. Luckily, they did not lose any of the horses, but Maria's favourite pony was quite badly burned, although he did survive. Ron came back and got his tractor and went down and stayed all day to help. Apparently the fire brigade said that it was started by someone walking past, and throwing a cigarette-end into the hay and straw shed, which was right by the road. How utterly thoughtless.

# SPLODGE

Cashel's Grace was a complete nutcase to ride and charged at every jump. She did not take kindly to schooling at all. It was quite nerve-racking; the only thing was that you knew she would never stop. Consequently she preferred cross-country to show jumping. Unfortunately, she still kept going even when slightly lame, and we could never ascertain the underlying cause. So we had to retire her from competing and she became a brood mare. The best foal she ever bred for me was by an Irish draught stallion called Kelly's Hero, a big dapple grey. The foal was born black but I was very pleased, as I knew she would turn grey in later life. She had her father's colouring but, oh boy, did she have her mother's temperament. She was very scatty! The filly was named Collingsdown Grace Kelly for obvious reasons.

When she was still a yearling and we had sent the mare back to stud, we decided we needed another horse to keep her company. Ron went to see our neighbour who always had some small ponies running in his fields, but apparently he had sold them, so he said that we could have his donkey. I was delighted, as I had always wanted a donkey. Goodness knows how old the donkey was, but Ron remembered her from our neighbour's previous home.

Ron walked her back to our home, but the poor thing had been neglected and her hooves were turning up at the ends, so it took them a long while to get home. We had our blacksmith come to see to her feet and it took several months to get them back into some sort of order, bless her. Anyway, she was turned out in the field with Splodge (one of her many names, because she had splodgy markings on her face during one aspect of her colour-changing life) while her mum went to stud, and they got on like a house on fire! Too well in fact – we could take Splodge away from the donkey (who became known as Didgeridoo – I don't know why – which was shortened to Didge) but you could not take Didge away from Splodge. A couple of times we had been out riding and Splodge and Didge were in the sand paddock. Didge had 'limbo-danced' under the railings and Splodge got in a big state and galloped down and jumped the railings to be out in the field with her. So, everything had to be made 'Didge-proof' – but all this turned out to be in our favour. You never really know what is around the corner!

One Saturday morning, Billy, Ron's workman who used to come out on Saturdays and clean out the stables, had taken hay down to the field and came back saying he thought that Splodge had broken her leg. We all dashed down and sure enough she was standing there with her leg straight out behind her. We realised that it was not a broken leg, but that her stifle joint had locked. We called the vet straight away, who did, indeed, confirm our thoughts and proceeded to put a rope around her fetlock, give a sharp tug and put the joint back in its place. He said that if it kept happening she would have to have a small operation on the ligaments that kept the stifle joint in place, as they were obviously loose. There was also the chance that she might grow out of it. Well, it did keep happening and although Ron could go down and attend to it and put it right each time we decided to go ahead and have the operation done on both stifle joints.

The operating theatre was in Holsworthy, and of course the filly had never been away from home let alone loaded in a horse trailer. What to do? A brilliant idea popped into my head: take Didge in as well. We had no problem loading Didge in the trailer, and of course Splodge would follow. I rang the veterinary practice and asked if it would be OK to do this and they said there was no problem with it as long as we realised that Didge would be starved the same as Splodge prior to the operation. Well, Didge was as fat as a mole and it certainly would not do her any harm. The day came, and Mr Barker arrived with the trailer. Didge walked up the ramp and Splodge duly followed. All was going according to plan! Didge stayed overnight with Splodge in her stable and walked into the pre-op room while Splodge was anaesthetised. Splodge had her operation and when she came round, who was there with her but Didge. When I spoke to the vet, he was very impressed and although he obviously thought I was a silly woman to start with, he said that it could not have gone smoother and it turned out to be a very good idea. And so Splodge's stifle joints never got stuck again.

Ron broke her in and she was a bit of a handful and thoroughly enjoyed bucking – the handstand sort! She was not my cup of tea to ride, and several of my friends had a go at riding her, but no one really liked her, as she was so unpredictable. She had a super jump in her, and Beccy, who was the daughter of the Mill Supervisor at work, said she would like to ride her, as her pony Sunny, was getting old. So Beccy used to come out after school. I would pick her up on the way home from work and either Ron or I would take her back home to Bideford. She was young and had no fear and jumped some really big jumps in the sand paddock. Even in the winter on dark evenings, as Ron rigged up some really strong lights and it was amazing to see the pair of them. Eventually, Beccy grew out of riding, and so I offered the mare to the daughter of my hairdresser. She had done her equine courses at Bicton and was working for someone in Rackenford and could not afford her own horse. So, Big Kel, as Splodge was also affectionately known as, went to Rackenford, after we had inspected it, of course, and proceeded to become a Grade C show jumper. Though, like her mother, her favourite discipline was cross-country, and also like her mother, she would never stop.

I think the trouble with show jumping and dressage (though she did quite a good test and went in several one day events) was that it was too controlled for her. Clare and Kelly got on very well together and she had her for five years. Ron and I would always go and support her whenever we could. She also won quite a lot in local Show Hunter and Handy Hunter classes, and won quite a lot with Clare. I don't really know why, but for some reason, eventually, Clare sent Kelly back home. My only regret is that while we always gave Clare some money when we went to support her to help to look after Splodge, Clare never gave me one of the rosettes that she had won (and she won a lot). I only have two and they were won by neighbours, who once took Splodge to a Bideford Riding Club summer show.

Beccy decided that she would like to come and ride her again, and so we went to many shows together in the next few years and again Splodge won a lot of rosettes. (I was riding Charlie who appears later in this book). When the mare was 17-years-old, Beccy said that she did not feel right to ride and she kept going slightly lame. We called the vet who said that she was too fat and a candidate for laminitis. We knew that this was not right as she was very fit and so, when there was no improvement, I called the vet again and had her feet X-rayed. The X-rays showed that her pedal bones were nearly through the bottom of her soles. This could mean that something was drastically wrong with her blood. We did what we could for her, by putting pads on her feet, but she looked very sorry for herself. Sadly, she had leukemia, which interfered with the blood supply to the walls of the feet and that is why her pedal bones sank. We sent the X-rays to the laminitis clinic, but the answer was the same. The mare was obviously experiencing horrendous pain and there was nothing that could be done.

There was no hope for remedial shoeing and so another awful Saturday arrived when we decided that we could not let Splodge suffer any longer. I had always hoped to breed from her, as I had from Grace, her mother, but life certainly has some horrid twists and turns and never ends up as you envisage!

# TWO OLD FRIENDS RETIRE TOGETHER

By 1987 my dear old Beauts was 25-years-old. Thanks to all the pounding about and cantering on the spot, and the awful habit that she had of kicking the water trough with her knee in hot weather so that the water splashed all over her face, life was always 'fun' with Beauts around! I remember one hot day at Holsworthy riding Club Summer Show, I had just finished a jumping round and took her up to the stone water trough to see if she was thirsty. She elegantly started sipping the water as most horses do until this rather posh partnership approached us, obviously with the same thing in mind. The Beauts went from sipping nicely to plunging her face in as far as it would go which was up to her eyes and, because it was a trough and she could, commenced 'swooshing' her face up and down lengthways. The other poor horse had a fit, shied and the poor woman nearly fell off, leaving me very red-faced, apologising profusely and saying, "Gosh that has never happened before, I wonder what got into her?" After that, I always made sure that Beauts did not drink from a trough with anyone else around at any shows that I went to. I was so embarrassed sitting on this horse with water dripping off her face and tack!

Beauts always fell in love with whichever horse she travelled to an event with. You could ride her away from her travelling companion, but you could not ride the other horse away from Beauts, not without dire consequences anyway. We had gone jumping at a local indoor school with Grace and Beauts and on this particular day, Grace had got into the 'jump off' and Beauty hadn't. As there were a lot of entries and the weather was not too good, we had put the horses back in the trailer as that was the only place to keep dry. At the appointed time, Val led Grace out of the trailer to warm up for the 'jump off' but Beauts was none too happy and began neighing rather loudly. We told her to be quiet but decided that she would come to no harm, so went into the school to watch Grace perform.

She was just coming to the end of her round when Mr Barker and I heard the most awful banging and crashing coming from outside. We both looked at one another and said, "Beauty!" and ran out from the school as fast as we could to see the great big, heavy, wooden Beaufort trailer rocking like it was going to capsize. Mr Barker dived through the small jockey door and luckily got there just as the Beauts was going to come over the breast bar. Val arrived outside the trailer with Grace just at that moment and Beauts somehow knew that Grace was there and immediately calmed down, and stood there like butter would not melt in her mouth. We never ever did that again. We always took Beauts out too, even if only on a halter, though she was ten times worse if she was in season.

Another time, we entered to compete at Cholwell, where there are two heavy sliding steel doors, which are shut behind you when you enter the ring, so no one waiting outside can see what's going on. Grace had gone in to jump and I was standing outside on Beauts, but she could hear Grace cantering around and jumping and every time she passed by on the inside of the doors Beauts would whicker. Suddenly there was complete silence and it was obvious that something had happened. Poor Beauty had her nose up to the crack in the door and the whinny soon turned into panicked braying, as she knew something had happened to her friend. Val had had an unfortunate fall but Beauty did not settle until the doors opened and she could see that Grace was okay.

I was very fortunate to have been able to hack, jump and enjoy Beauty for eleven years, but her aforementioned habit of kicking the water trough to cool her face down in hot weather (or whenever she felt like it, just because she could) was her undoing. Her knee became big and calloused. I had the vet out to have a look at it and he said that she had bursitis of the knee, and that I could ride her but not jump her because she would lose flexion in her knee. I hacked her for a little while longer, but one Thursday evening, while I was out just walking down the road, I could hear her scraping her toes in the ground so I pulled up and jumped off (I could in those days!) and sadly led her back home knowing that the time had come to retire her. I only sat on her twice more after that day and both were hair-raising experiences. Once, I put her bridle on when she was in the sand paddock. I rode her to the end, which was fine, but the minute I turned at the bottom she took off, bucking. So when she finally stopped, I got off. The last time was in the winter of 1987. We had a very cold spell and the ice was six inches thick on the fishpond.

## TWO OLD FRIENDS RETIRE TOGETHER

Ron had to saw a circle in the ice to let the oxygen in so that the fish would not die. We were not able to get the horses out of the stable as the yard was too icy and it just did not 'give' at all, so we decided that the horses were safer in their stables, even if they were busting a gut. When the thaw started, we decided to lead the horses down the road, as they would have gone mental if we let them out into the field, and anyway, the field had not defrosted properly. I decided I would ride Beauts bareback instead of leading her, which as another mistake because it was still dangerously icy. Away from home she walked very well, but the minute she was turned back she did her normal explosion. So the Beauts and Grace, who were two great friends, were retired together for ten years and eight years respectively.

Years later, I went out one morning at 5.30am, as I could hear a banging sound coming from the stables and saw that Grace was down in her box. I dashed in and got Ron and he came out and tried to get her up. She made a tremendous effort but could not make it, so there was no decision to make. I went inside and phoned for the vet. One of my favourites – Jane – came out. I stayed in the kitchen, as I always want to remember my horses as they were in life. On Jane's way out she came into me and said that I had made the right decision, as if we had managed to get her up it would only happen again and that would not have been fair on her – so that made me feel somewhat better. I then went off to work, and Ron made the arrangements to bury her in one of our fields.

Two years later I noticed that Beauty was 'listing' to one side and was walking in a circle. Ron came and had a look at her and said that he thought that she pulled some muscles and gave her some treatment. I then called the vet and he said that he was sure that she had had a slight stroke, gave her some medication and said leave her for a week to see if there was any improvement, but there was none. He asked us what we wanted to do and pointed out that if she lay down at all she would not be able to get up again. Well, I couldn't bear that and so we had another horrible decision to make. We made the arrangement for the vet to come on Saturday morning, so I went out on Lancer with the girls and Ron stayed with Beauts. He always maintained that she was the worst horse that he had ever known (that was only because she was the only horse that got the better of him), but when it came to that fateful morning, he was in tears. I got back from my ride and Ron had made all the arrangements and so she was buried with her friend Grace. The end of another era.

# LANCER

So now I was on the lookout for yet another horse. That meant the *Western Morning News* every day, although Wednesdays and Fridays were the really horsey days, but by now the paper had turned into a tabloid and there were only one or two columns as opposed to the one or two pages that there used to be, making looking for a horse part of the fun. Times they are a-changing, and fast. My penchant for greys reared its ugly head again and I spotted a dapple grey gelding for sale in St Austell. I rang and enquired and was told that he was very good in traffic and in stable but liked to "go on a bit". For some unknown reason I asked what he was called and was told his name was Lancer. I mentioned Lancer to Ron, but he said he said that he thought that St Austell was rather a long way to go and so to forget it. This was in August and I looked at the paper at every available moment but at this time of year, there seemed nothing much for sale. I went to see Brian at Lostwithiel, who was a 20-year-old ex-Grade C show jumper. They wanted a £1000 with tack,, which I thought was a bit much. Poor thing, he had a 'snobby' nose and could not be kept on straw as he was allergic to it, and when I rode him he went lame. So that was the end of that.

In October, another grey gelding was advertised for sale, but much nearer to home this time, and so I thought that I might go and have a look. He was at Crackington Haven and so Ron and I went over one Saturday lunchtime. The owner of the establishment was there and was getting ready to go hunter trialing the next day. She told me that she had bought the gelding from a horse sale in Exeter in the previous August and that his name was Lancer. 'Doing!' Lights started going off in my head: it had to be the same horse! This was 'meant to be' I thought. Lancer was in his stable, backside to the door, munching on hay. We went in and he wasn't at all bothered and took the peppermints that I offered him with gusto. He was tacked-up and I was advised to take him down the road on my own, I was assured he would be absolutely fine, as kids who worked at the stable had ridden him on the cliffs, on rides and at gymkhanas. So, off I went. He was as good as gold as we went down the quiet, narrow country lanes, but all of a sudden the silence was shattered by silly old woman driver coming round the bend with her hand on the motor horn going full blast. Lancer never batted an eyelid and so we went on a bit further before turning round and going back. Ron and the owner were a bit apprehensive, as they had heard the horn and wondered what had happened, but all was well. He was then schooled and jumped round the ménage to show me how good he was.

We left with me saying that I would think it over and ring later in the evening. I decided that I would have Lancer and rang back in the evening as I said I would. The owner seemed very surprised when I said that I would have him. "Are you sure?" she said. We left it that Mr Barker would go down and collect him the following Wednesday. Her parting remark was, "If you ever need any help riding him, just give me a ring." I thought it was a bit of a peculiar thing to say. Alarm bells should have rung, and I was soon to find out why the remark was made. I was rung two days before Mr Barker was due to collect Lancer to say that they had to come near to where I was living and if I liked, they would deliver Lancer for £10. Again, alarm bells should have rung but I just thought, "Oh, that's nice, and will save me some money" and so I agreed.

They got lost on the way and rung home as I was waiting eagerly for my new steed to be delivered. They had pulled into a lay-by near Stibb Cross and so I suggested that I would come out and 'guide them in' as it seemed that most people could not find their way to our property unless they knew the area. I did so and, wow, did he look lovely when he emerged from the trailer. They had obviously bathed him, pulled his mane, and he was rugged and bandaged. I had booked the following morning off of work so that I could go riding on him. My friend came out and we went out for an hour together and had a lovely time. From then on things went downhill.

He turned out to be the most jumpy and nervy horse that I had ever ridden in my life. He would 'splat' regularly, (which is the only word I can find to describe his jumpy nervousness at anything – or usually nothing – in the hedge). If he did it once, he did it ten times, and that would be on a good day, if I was lucky. I now understood the parting remark from his previous owner, but there was no way I was going to ask for help to ride him, as pride would not let me – but in reality, I didn't think that much help could be given anyway. He had a lovely temperament in the stable and was brilliant in traffic, but in the great wide outdoors he was petrified of things that weren't there, and that was the way he remained for the ten years that I had him.

I did love him, though, and my only regret was that I could not take him to any shows and jump him. Ron is convinced that he was either drugged or had had his water stopped (as that would have the desired affect of making him quiet) on the day that we went to see him and the day that he was delivered. I tend to believe him. I had not had him very long and Mr Barker was going to take us indoor show jumping at Cholwell. I 'tarted' him up, plaiting his mane, and bandaging his legs properly with gamgee and the red looked lovely on his colouring. Mr Barker arrived and we got Lancer and Laddie out to load. Not anticipating any problem, I tried to load Lancer and he backed out of the trailer and did not appear to like it. Val then loaded Laddie who just stood there in the trailer, as he was used to it. I then loaded Lancer who came straight out again at such a rate that his back legs collapsed under him and he skinned both his hocks down to the bone. Well, that obviously put an end to our show jumping sojourn for the day and evermore really. He was just so frightened of everything. I was lucky really that in the ten years that I rode him I only came off him four times. All because of his shying.

I had not had him long and was galloping him over the moor when he shied at nothing, quite badly, and I was just thinking, "Thank god, sat that," when he immediately shied the other way and threw me off completely. I was only 40 then so I just let go, bounced and rolled out of the way of the flying hooves. Of course, not having had Lancer long, I was worried about him. He did have the sense to gallop back in the direction of home, albeit down the main road. I just shouted to my friend to get him and that I was okay. I picked myself up, absolutely seething about the fact that I had come off, and at what Lancer had done. I was storming down the road – I had about a mile and a half trek back home – when a car came up the road and stopped and said, "Your friend had caught your horse. Would you like a lift down to him?" As usual, and not putting my brain into gear because I was so mad, I said, "No, thank you!" through gritted teeth. It was just as well, as I wanted to get all the anger out of my system. When I finally reached them, I re-mounted and we recommenced our ride. Apart from a few shies he was okay, but now I had learnt my lesson, almost.

He was always so unpredictable and shied at things that nobody else could see. I was cantering along the grass on a bank and jumped a ditch – we had been along this stretch umpteen times and he had always been okay – when suddenly, as we were jumping, he shied on take-off and I went sailing through the air and landed in the middle of the road. I rolled and got up. Val asked if I was okay and I asked her to just catch that horse. She caught him and I got on 'shaken but not stirred' (well not much anyway). Val thought I would want to 'limp home and lick my wounds' but I wanted to see what he had shied at. It was a pile of stones that had not been there the day before when we had passed the same spot.

When I got home, I told Ron, who happened to be doing some work for the owner of the farm where the incident occurred, and Ron said that he had put the stones there that day! I have since found out that a mound of stones can look like it is moving and rippling (you learn something every day, sometimes the hard way, literally in my case) and my poor horse must have been alert to this. When we used to get back home after a ride, as we turned off the road and into the gateway to go into the yard and I stopped him to get off, he always let out a huge sigh – a sigh of relief that everything was okay, no doubt.

I rode him for ten years and luckily only came off of him another three times. Once, jumping him in the sand paddock. That was Ron's fault, because he said that he would never stop. Well, he did, on take-off stride but I landed on my feet, got on again – very mad – blaming no-one but myself and vowing never to listen to Ron's advice again, even though the bottom line was it was my fault as I was riding him! Another time in the field, I had been jumping him in the sand paddock and Ron said he thought he would go better in the field, so we set up a course there. Wrong! I think he was afraid of the wide-open spaces. Trust me to have a horse with agoraphobia! The third time was Good Friday. A friend Tessa and I had gone out for a ride across the moor, and were riding over there talking away, when she suddenly said (because she knew what Lancer was like), "Mind the ph…" That was all I heard. The next minute I was doing an impression of a helicopter and landed in the ditch on the left hand side of the road. After discovering that I was okay, Tessa told me she was trying to say, "Mind the pheasant" but the warning didn't get to me before the pheasant got to Lancer! I just had saw Lancer galloping off home and Tessa galloping after him. I told her not to chase him but I don't think she could stop, and so there I was again, stomping up the road with my crop in my hand, absolutely livid. Ron came down the road in the car and when he saw me, he laughed his head off. I harrumphed into the passenger seat and we drove home where I was re-united with my steed and started the ride again. This time I managed it without further ado!

I got used to riding Lancer and took no notice of his shies, although he used to frighten riders and pedestrians alike. As I've mentioned earlier, we had a moor about half a mile down the road and it is common land, so we used to ride over it and make jumps etc. and generally enjoy ourselves. I don't know how it happened, but a local farmer whose ground backed onto the moor claimed the land and it then became fenced off. We could no longer ride on it, and then it became obvious that animals were going to be kept in it. We had bullocks on one side and these were always nutty and galloped up to the fence, which used to scare Lancer a bit, but not too badly as he could see what they were. On the other side were sheep, which was not too bad for a while, until the farmer put a 'lamb creep 'in the field. Oh my god!

Poor Lancer was absolutely petrified; the lamb creep was an ancient wooden affair and the bars were facing away from the road so all that poor Lancer could see was a lot of legs prancing about inside, not attached to bodies. It must have looked like a very weird creature to him. I managed to get him passed it several times, though he always got very wound up coming down to it. Poor chap – he cracked completely one evening ride. We had gone past said place on the way out for our ride, with no problem, but on the way home he suddenly took off and shot straight toward the barbed-wire fence on the left hand side of the road. Well, I just sat there and thought, "Here goes then!" because I really thought he was going to jump it, but instead he pinged off of it and I managed to pull him up, but there was no way he was going to go on. I tried everything you could think of but he was petrified (again of something that I could not see. I only wish I could have got inside his head). I didn't try and lead him because I knew that he would pull away and I would not be able to hold on to him. There was only one thing for it – the long way home. It put another four miles on the ride, but we trotted on and came back around in a big circle and down the main road. I did ride him a few times afterwards but could never take him down past the moor again. Time to retire the old boy and look for another horse.

One thing I want to mention about Lancer is that I had bought him as a 10-year-old, but on inspecting his teeth, I'm sure he was much older than that. Throughout my life with horses, I have done a study of the teeth of all the horses that I have had as they have always ended their days with us. Actually knowing a horse's age when we have either bred or bought them, (as they are all passported now), has made things a lot easier and I think that Lancer must have been at least 20-years-old when I had him. Not that I regret having him as he taught me quite a lot, and he is the only horse that I have never had to call a vet to see. Lancer had been retired and on his final day about two years later we went out for a drink on a Sunday lunchtime and my last memory of Lancer is him trotting across the field to the hedge looking a bit 'wide eyed and legless' as he could hear something going on and he went across to see what it was. It was the neighbouring farmer's sheepdogs in there. When we came back about two hours later, Lancer was dead in the sand paddock. Ron covered him with a tarpaulin before we could get him buried the next day. I think he must have had a massive heart attack, as there had been no signs of illness beforehand, so I just hope that he did not suffer and it was over in an instant.

So, now began my quest for yet another horse....

# QUEEN'S CHAPLAIN – AKA CHARLIE

I let the aforementioned Dave (of bucking young horse fame) know that I was looking for another horse and he said he would keep an eye out for me. When he was at the stud that belonged to his friend and they were out exercising stallions, he had one of those light bulb moments and said to his friend, "I know of just the horse for Ann" to which Graham said, "Oh yes, which one?" Dave said, "You're sitting on it!" The horse was (I was told) a 16.hh Irish Thoroughbred who was 13-years-old. Raced over hurdles and steeplechase fences and very well bred by The Parson, he had won a bit of money and Graham had bought him for his daughter to point-to-point. He was a superb looking horse but he'd had a crashing fall at Haydock and the jockey had broken his leg and then he really didn't like jumping any more. Graham thought that a bit of hunting would sweeten him up and then he would race again. Alas for Graham, he was wrong – but his bad luck, I am glad to say, was my good luck! The only drawbacks for me was that I couldn't expect him to jump a coloured pole and I had to watch him when I did the girth up, as he had actually picked the Whipper-In up when he got off to do the girth and deposited him in the hedge! Both of these things I could live with, especially as I liked getting horses going again that had stopped jumping. I enjoy a challenge!

Apparently Charlie would go to point-to point and look fabulous and would start the race well, but after the third fence he would pull himself out of the race and stop jumping all together. Graham, who was Master of the Stevenstone Foxhounds, then decided that, as he had him he would use him as a Huntmaster's horse or for the Whipper-In. Dave came over one Saturday morning in November and said that he had arranged for us to go up to see Charlie on Sunday and that he would go out for a ride with me, but if we wanted to see him prior to that, he was out hunting and he told us where they had met. There followed a frantic race across country, and everywhere we ended up the hounds had just moved on and so we never got to see him in action.

Sunday morning arrived and it was normal west-country November weather, blowing a gale and pouring with rain and nobody in their right mind would be going out looking at horses in it, but of course I am not in my right mind and there was no way I was going to miss it for the world. Especially not this close to home: normally I had to go all over the country to find the right horse and even then, ended up disappointed! We picked up Dave on the way through Langtree and went on to High Bickington, parked the car at the stud and followed Dave – who seemed to know where he was going – and came to a small narrow stable. A beautiful horse's head was looking out and Dave opened the door and we all squeezed in. I was aghast at the height and said, "Blow me David (or words to that effect), I thought you said he was 16.hh?" A little voice piped up from behind Charlie's back legs (this was Graham giving him a brush down after the previous day's hunting, and who was completely out of sight). "He's 16.3hh but if David says he's 16.hh – he's 16.hh." The small stable made him look even bigger to me. I looked at David sternly, and he said, "Well, if I had told you he was 16.3hh you would not have come to see him!" (Little did he know, but I had learnt through my life looking at horses that they never were the height that you thought they were going to be because basically people did not measure them or they add some inches put on or in my present case taken off! I'd learned to keep open-minded in this respect.)

It was still blowing a gale and pouring with rain when we got the horses out (Dave had borrowed one to accompany me), and I climbed on to a wall to mount. For some reason, the stirrups were jockey level and very short (I expect Rebecca had been riding him), so I said, "Oh heck, I can't ride like this!" But the weather was so bad I couldn't even be bothered to mess around and change the length of the stirrups even though I do like to ride very long. Graham said to Ron, "I think it's about time we went in for a coffee!"

Ducks would not even have gone out in that weather, but when we came back like drowned rats (after about half an hour) I did not want to get off Charlie. I had fallen in love with him. I did eventually get off of course, un-tacked, made sure Charlie was okay and then David and I squelched into the kitchen to scrounge a cup of something to warm up. Ron asked how I had got on and I said great and that I would definitely have him – as I dripped everywhere in Lynn's kitchen. Graham then said, "Well, if you have him…" – I said, "He's sold!" – Graham continued, "if you have him…" – I cut him off again and said. "He's sold!!" – and Ron said, "I think he's sold Graham. Your next meet is at Stowford (a mile from us) so I should hunt him and drop him off when you have finished." "Not likely," said Graham. "That horse stays in his box until Tuesday night when I will bring him out to you. Knowing my luck, I'll hunt him and he'll break a leg or something!"

He did actually have a 'big front leg' big' (horse parlance) on that Sunday and Graham said he had knocked it in the box, but I knew that was not right. When I came back from riding him the swelling in the leg had gone right down, so as far as I was concerned it was not too serious and I was quite happy that I could cope with it. In my opinion it looked like he had a windgall on the leg and that was probably another reason why he did not like jumping, as it would have been painful for him.

So, Tuesday 11th November, I took possession of Queen's Chaplain and what a phenomenal horse he turned out to be, and still is for that matter. Funnily enough we were in The Clinton Arms at Frithelstock having a drink one evening – indeed it used to be a pub that we frequented a lot forty two years ago and I also used to work behind the bar back then – and there was a man there who I had never seen before, but Ron knew him he was the 'Whipper In' with the hunt, the very one that Charlie had picked up with his teeth and deposited in the hedge. Ever since, poor Charlie's stable name at the Kennels had been Goofy, because of his teeth.

We told him that we had Charlie now, and he said, "Good luck!" I got the impression that he did not like Charlie too much, not only because of the teeth and hedge episode, but also he would not jump anything for him. He said I would never get him to jump a coloured pole, as he would not even jump an eighteen inch pole out hunting (and usually horses will jump anything in hot blood and not jump in cold blood – by which I mean they follow the crowd out hunting and even the worst jumper will go over anything just to keep up with the other horses). Red rag to a bull time again. Another challenge! I am pleased to say that I have proved him wrong!

Charlie and I get on like a house on fire and I did manage to get him jumping again. Our first venture was in Hartland where I had second thoughts about what I would achieve. We went into the Clear Round Jumping and as he did not know what he was doing, it was very difficult to keep him straight at a jump. He jumped the first one and stopped at the second then cat jumped it. He sent me skywards. I did a pirouette and landed on my feet, but I came down from such a great height that I can remember thinking, "Oh my poor knees!" as I watched the ground approaching – luckily I sank onto my derrière! I looked round and Charles was nonchalantly eating grass. I burst into laughter. Someone caught him then found Ron and said, "You had better come quick - Ann has fallen off." When I picked myself up and was walking out of the ring, the steward said, "If you want to take him round again I will pay for you." How nice. I said, "Don't worry, I am going again but I have to get on first and the only way I can is on a mounting block!" I had brought one in the lorry. I had one for Lancer too as he was bigger than Beauty, and then Ron had to make me a bigger one to mount Charlie. I am like a boy scout; I always come prepared!

Charlie had tested me out again not long after I had bought him, as they very often do. Tessa and I left the yard and were about ten yards down the road when Charles decided he was not going on! I 'asked' him nicely then I 'told' him with some smacks down the shoulder, and he still was not having it, so unfortunately the crop had to come into play 'seriously'. Every time I smacked him behind the saddle he bucked, or rather fly-kicked (all on the spot, he was just registering his displeasure, not trying to dislodge me in any way) and I told him matter-of-factly that one of us is going to give in and it is not going to be me! Luckily for me, I got it right and he stopped and walked on then as if nothing had happened. From that day we have had a terrific relationship and one of my proudest moments was his first rosette – a 2nd for show jumping at The Grange near Okehampton – and this on a horse that was "never going to jump a coloured pole", and ridden by an 53-year-old who never thought she would be lucky enough to grace a show jumping arena again!

We went jumping on a lot of occasions and the older he got the nuttier he became to ride and ended up bucking and squealing when the bell went to start, so he really enjoyed it. He liked indoor jumping (again because of the soft going) so I did not jump him outside much because of his leg and the only time he ever put in a stop was outside. It was a baking hot day and the ground was rock hard. I felt him backpedalling from the first, so I made him jump once, but then pulled him out. And so I spent thirteen happy years hacking and jumping Charlie. Then Ron thought that I ought to retire him as he was a 'classy' Thoroughbred and they tend to get old quite quickly and he had had a hard life up until he was 13-years-old, so I bowed to Ron's superior knowledge and was on the lookout for yet another horse! (I never realised how many horses I had ridden or bought until I started writing this book!)

# PIRATE

Seeing as David had found me such a wonderful horse in 1997, I told him that Ron thought I ought to retire Charlie and I asked him again if he would keep his eyes and ears open for me again. I was hoping that lightning would strike twice, but unfortunately it did not. Dave came one Saturday and told me of a horse that was approximately 12-years-old and had been hunting on Exmoor. This sounded absolutely perfect: the right age so that he should know what life is all about, and old enough to have got over any teething problems. Dave arranged to take us over to Rose Ash near South Molton to see him and so that I could try him out. He was in a stall in a big barn and tied up. The owner went and put the bridle on him and then the saddle and said he would ride him first. He rode the horse up the lane, and the horse seemed a bit 'joggy'. Then he went down the road and I thought he looked unsound – then he came up the road and I could see that indeed he was, so obviously there was no way I could try out an unsound horse. I told them I liked the look of him and they said that they would get the blacksmith in to look at his foot. I did notice that he also had a windgall but was not too worried (as we had managed Charlie's) and that is how he presented.

The owners said that the blacksmith could find nothing wrong with his foot and that I could have Pirate on loan for as long as I wanted and so I thought I would take the chance. They delivered him later that week. Well, those first months were awful! He did nothing but kick the stable door to get out even though he was in an American barn with Charlie beside him who he could see through mesh and another pony across from him. His temperament, too, was very suspect: ears back all the time, kicking and swishing his tail, and dunging all the time, most of which was like a cow!

He also had a hogged mane (a 'lazy man's mane' which is clipped short) and as I don't like them we let it grow out and my friend said he looked like 'Mr T'. I said, then "No, more like Mr 'P'" and so that stuck! It suited everything about him, Mr Pain, Mr Pooh... He was a pain in more ways than one, as I found out when I tried to get the bridle on him. He would not open his mouth! He also stuck his head in the air so that I couldn't reach. The first thing I did was to change his bit as they had ridden him in a twisted snaffle, which to me is one of the most severe bits that you can get and must have felt awful. I always ride in a jointed eggbutt snaffle, so whatever a horse has arrived with, I always try them in the snaffle first of all. I was at a display once by Graham Fletcher and he said if you can't ride in a snaffle don't bother! I have always remembered that.

It took ages to get the bridle on and I had to have Ron come in and twitch him by the ear. However, once saddled up he behaved himself impeccably, even if he was not a comfortable ride as he was so unbalanced. Dave came out the next weekend to see how he was going and when I told him about the problem with the bridle he scoffed and said he would put it on. It took him fifty minutes as we left him to it on his own. It was then slipped into the conversation that Mr P wasn't broken in until he was 9-years-old! I later found out that he had only been hunted about twice as he always came back unsound. So, it became quite obvious that although nobody had told any lies, it wasn't exactly the whole truth either. So, poor old Charlie came out of retirement and I rode one on Saturday and one on Sunday trying to get the windgall right.

Twice I was going to send him back, as I was really tired of hearing him kicking the door in his impatience, coupled with the problem with the bridle, but his one saving grace was that he was so good to ride. He was very green, and needed a lot of work, but traffic proof, and he was improving all the time as a 'ride'. I persevered, and it wasn't long before I could get the bridle on unaided (unless he had one of his moments). He settled down and palled-up with Charlie. He had a bout of lameness where I couldn't ride him for six weeks and worryingly, he did not pass the navicular test. I put him on Devil's Claw as it is the natural answer to the veterinary remedy of bute. Nonetheless, I thought I had better look for another horse as the prognosis for Mr P did not look good if, indeed, it turned out that he had navicular. Charlie was now back as my ride, I loved it and so did he, whilst, yes you've guessed it, I looked for another horse.

# BRIGHT SPRYNGH

Truth be known, I actually did have another horse. She was a chestnut mare, 16.2hh. Like everything in my life, I came about her in an unusual way. Tess had just lost Dessie, her horse, and was on the lookout for another horse or pony (or rather I was on her behalf). I saw a horse advertised near Exeter for sale or loan and so she wanted to go down and see her. Bright Spryngh she was called, but ws known as Bea. She was an Irish Sports Horse and I was assured, had been ridden by a novice and was also a novice ride. So, Tessa and I went down to Exeter bright and early one Sunday morning. I stayed behind while Tessa went for a short hack with Rebecca, her owner, and she came back full of smiles and decided that she would have her on a month's trial, which was fine with us. I was in the bath the next Sunday morning when Bea arrived. Ron came in and said he had to get away quick, as he had put a nice feed in for the horse, seeing as the mare had travelled up such a long way, but Rebecca had said, "Get that out of the trough, it is not tea-time yet!" Tessa had a contract as thick as a book to sign, with what she could and couldn't do, and what she could and couldn't feed the horse.

Rebecca came up to see her in the middle of the month to check that everything was as it should be, and was delighted with the stables and how she was being looked after. Tessa rode her for a month alongside me, and we mostly walked and trotted, but on the last day we had a canter, which was uphill. I thought that Tessa would be able to manage her but Bea got faster and faster and I was having a struggle on Charlie behind as he thought we were going racing. I knew that the only thing I could do was keep back as far as I could and when the mare knew I wasn't behind her, Tess would be able to stop her, which she did, but it had frightened her. We walked all the way home but sadly, Tess did not want to keep her.

Ron and I had a talk about it and decided that as the mare had settled in we would buy her, and so after a drink in the local hostelry (which seems to be involved in a lot of my stories) I called Tessa and said that we would buy her so that she needn't make arrangements to take her back to Exeter. Tess was delighted as we all liked the mare, and she thought Rebecca would be glad. Well, she wasn't. She told me that as Tess had rung and said that she didn't want her, she had an excited 15-year-old waiting to try her out the next day. I kept my temper, as I thought she would want us to have her as it was a good home and also I pointed out that the excited 15-year-old would soon turn into a moody 18-year-old who was into boys and also would probably go to University – and as the mare was quite old, you could not guarantee what sort of a home she would get, whereas she would have one for life with us. I really could not have cared one way or the other, but then Rebecca saw the light and agreed that we could buy her. I never got to ride her much, as Laddie was getting old and was about to be retired and as I was riding Charlie and

I really didn't need another horse, so my friend Val started to ride her and continued to do so for the six years that I had her. I did get to ride her twice, but Val loved her and so I could not take the mare away from her.

# DARCO

Before I went back to the papers and Internet in my search for another horse, I let Dave know, just in case he did hear of a horse for sale – and he did ring me to say that he knew of one near High Bickington. "Oh well, worth a punt," I thought as it was so close to us, but it turned out that was not the case. It again illustrates how careful one has to be when trying and buying horses. I was told that Darco (as we referred to him because he was similar to the show jumper of that name) he was 17.1hh, had been with same people since a youngster, had point-to-pointed, hunted, was 17-years-old and looking for a good home for £900. The farmer's wife just rode him round the fields at home. As we are always suckers for any animal looking for a good home, we went to see him.

He was in a small stable and looked huge. He was a lovely black colour and had a lovely temperament so I said that I would have him for a week or two and see how I got on with him. What could go wrong? Hunted and point-to-pointed, he must've definitely known about life (NOT!) The farmer brought him over to us, but when we put him the stable he didn't seem to know what the feed trough was. He was petrified of it. When he got used to it he liked it and ate quite well. Ron put him in the sand paddock and he jumped out of it, as I think Mr P was a bully and terrified him. We let him settle in for a week and when we thought that he was used to the other horses, I decided I would take him out for a ride on the Saturday morning. I groomed him (good as gold), tacked him up (good as gold), but when I got him out of the stable and to the mounting block he was a quivering wreck. He would not stand still and went round and round the mounting block. I was not going to be outdone and somehow managed to mount the 'whirling dervish' that was Darco.

We jogged off down the road with Val and Tessa in our wake. When I got to about two hundred yards down the lane, he started leaping from one side of the road to the other. There was a ditch on both sides and one side also had a loose barbed wire fence and I was slightly fearful of getting caught up in it. I then decided that this was never going to work and somehow managed to get him to stand still for a nanosecond while I jumped off. I had heck of a job to lead him back as he walked all over me and pushed me into the hedge (a 5'1" human and a 17.1hh frightened horse do not go together) and he didn't calm down until I had put him back into his stable. I tacked up Mr P, left a note for Ron to explain what had happened and then went for a ride, but was very upset. I can only come to the conclusion that I had been trying to ride an agoraphobic horse. When I rang Dave and told him, again the truth came out. He hadn't actually been to a Meet, he had just joined in when the hunt was near, and the wife's sister had taken him away to her home to ride him but he didn't settle. Everyone had thought that as he had got older he would be quieter and more amenable, but my experience of horses is that as they get older they get nuttier. Poor chap. I felt really sorry for him, as he was such a lovely animal, but too old to do anything with now I fancy. They were disappointed that I didn't have him but came and took him back and so he will retire on the farm that he had been on all his life. I was just so glad that no traffic had come along. So, take note all you purchasers of horses. Never believe everything that anyone tells you about their steed, and be very careful! Even people who have bought horses for many years and think they know most things about horses, don't!

# JACK

So it was back to the papers, and now I had the Internet as well. I went down to Newton Abbot to see Louis, but the weather was so bad I did not ride him. Even though he was nice, he was a bit too wide for my liking. The next outing was interesting: 'The horse that never was!' – and just shows how unscrupulous dealers can be. I saw on the Internet 'Rupert' advertised by a man that I knew was a dealer in Cornwall, together with a picture. He sounded just my 'cup of tea', a 16.3hh Irish Thoroughbred, "good in every way," and only £1800. I rang and spoke to said dealer and he agreed that Rupert sounded just what I was looking for. I then rang Dave, as I knew he was an acquaintance, and he said that if this person said the horse was okay, then it was. Dave later rang me to say that he had actually rung the dealer and they both agreed that it was the horse for me! I arranged to go down the next morning and set off early as we had a long way to go. When we got to the establishment, the owner walked up to us and I said we had come to see Rupert. "Oh, he's sold," he said. "He was sold last week, but I have some others that you might be interested in".

Slightly miffed, to say the least, we followed him down to some stables in a barn where he showed us quite a nice dappled grey (right up my street). He told us it was his wife's horse, and I remember wondering if she knew he was being offered for sale. I was quite interested, so I asked the price. "Three," he said. "What?" I asked, astounded, "*three thousand pounds!*" and at that, I gave the horse a pat on the neck said "No thanks!" and stomped off in the haughtiest manner I could muster. We had gone all that way for nothing. I proceeded to chew-off Dave's ear on the way home and ended up in the local hostelry to drown my sorrows and calm myself down!

Back to the Internet! I saw a horse called Jack advertised for sale near Winkleigh which at least, was not so far to go. I phoned them and made arrangements to go and see him the following day. Jack was kept in a barn with another chestnut who kept biting chunks out of him. Apparently the owner had had him for seven years but was giving up riding, and said that he hadn't been ridden for the last six months. I took one look and fell in love with him: he was nearly black with a big white blaze. I asked Chloe, the owner, to trot him up the road, which she did, and I could see that he was sound. When she came back I said I would have him. Chloe was gob-smacked and asked whether I wanted to ride him. I explained that I only wanted to see him move. I asked if she wanted cash or cheque, shook hands and left after telling her I would ring in the week when I had made arrangements to get Jack home. I rang Dave and asked if he could fetch Jack for me, and we went the following Sunday. Chloe said he might be difficult to load as he hadn't been in a trailer for a long time (though he had been hunting, show jumping and supposedly raced as a youngster!) Anyway, he loaded in ten seconds and was as good as gold all the way home. Chloe's mother told me later that Chloe was upset as she thought that I was a dealer (ha ha!) as I hadn't wanted to try him out. I told her nothing could be further from the truth and that if I couldn't ride a horse now at my age, I never would. And so, Jack came home to our stables.

He was naughty with the bridle to start with, which I found funny as he would stick his bum in your face and just swing around the box away from you, from corner to corner with a cheeky look on his face. He basically has a nice temperament, but had just been allowed to get away with things! He, again, was very green, but I have had him for eighteen months now and am gradually knocking him in to shape. My main problem is that I can only ride at weekends and only then as long as the weather is not icy or gale force winds, and the last few winters have been getting colder and icier (I thought we were supposed to be experiencing global warming!) In reality, I don't think that he had been ridden in a couple of years as he was very cold-backed to get the saddle on, and his back was very weak. The first time I asked him to walk-on, his back legs nearly collapsed underneath him. It was all very strange as he felt like he was going to sit down, but he has quite a nice top-line now.

# TINTERN MEMORY

Ron came home from work one day and said that he was buying a horse from a good friend of ours Liz, whom he did a lot of work for. She had been a very good rider in her day, and had won at Eventing, in Show Classes at fairly high-class local shows, and she even had had a couple of good race horses. Some years ago, her husband, John (who had always been ill as long as I had known him), had very bad kidney trouble. He bought Lizzie a foal just before he went to a hospital in Tintern to have an operation. Sadly, he died and Lizzie named the foal after the hospital where he died, and so the foal was registered as Tintern Memory. Ron had been working at her farm and she had said that things were getting tough for her and that she wanted to sell some horses. Tintern was never broken-in, only bred from, and so as we had lost Gracie and no longer had L'Oreal, we decided to buy Tintern. She was a lovely light bay mare about 16.2hh. She had a lovely temperament but had never been taught any manners and at 8-years-old it was a bit late to start teaching her! You could just about get a halter on her, but trying to lead her somewhere that she did not want to go was a nightmare. It is very difficult trying to contain half a ton of horseflesh when it wants to go in a different direction to the designated one! But, as we were only going to breed from her it was probably not going to matter too much.

She was a very well bred mare by Cruise Missile and her grandmother was a very good west-country point-to-pointer. To breed from Tintern, we decided to use an Irish Draught stallion, Tobias Corbett, who was standing at a local stud, mainly because we thought that we should like to try and breed an eventer. Tobias was a beautiful liver chestnut, combining all the best qualities of the true Irish Draught: a stallion with very correct conformation and athletic movement. It has been said by some experts in the field that Tobias Corbett is one of the finest examples of the Irish Draught horse this side of the Irish Sea, being bred as he is by Slyguff Hero, who is full brother to King of Diamonds. Tobias Corbett has produced nice looking horses with good jumping ability and has produced foals which have won at Devon County, Bath & West, Malvern etc. In 2002, he produced the champion foal at the Irish Draught Breed Society Show. He produces bold forward going horses with a tremendous jump. None of the above really does this handsome stallion justice – but as I write this book, he is sadly deceased.

Tintern's first foal we called Tintern Toby, as we had decided that we would like to keep the Tintern name going. He got to 17.2hh and was quite a big boy. Ron broke him in and when he was a 3-year-old, I had the stupid idea that I could "ride him on" – as I was around 55 at the time it really was silly! He was huge! I used to come back from a Saturday morning hack and then take Toby out with my friend Beccy riding her little coloured pony that she was keeping with us.

Toby was very strong and cantankerous and used to try and turn and go home, and it took both hands on one rein to get him out of the hedge. (See what I mean? Silly!) Well, we went around the block on one of our Saturday rides and we were going to have a canter on the grass verge, which was higher than road level. I don't know what happened but I was suddenly catapulted up into the air and next thing I knew, I was 'splat' in the middle of the road, spread-eagled like a star-fish. Beccy asked if I was okay and I said yes and tried to get up. I managed it, but I could not stand on my left leg and the pain was tremendous, so I obviously could not get back on Toby again. Luckily, some nice people came along in a car and took me the mile home, and Beccy led Toby and the pony back. I gradually got stiffer and stiffer by the time I went to bed. It took me nearly fifteen minutes with Ron helping me to get up the stairs whilst yelling in pain. It was such agony. Of course, I did not go to the doctor as what could they do? Next morning I was worse and I could only get to the bathroom on my hands and knees. Ron found a 'gazunda' and I had that in the bedroom. I was in bed for a week and when I got out, Ron had the brilliant idea of using a stool like a Zimmer frame so that I could get around, and so that is what I did. Before too long, it was only taking five minutes to negotiate the stairs.

I was dying to get back in the saddle again to see whether the fall had affected my attitude to riding, but I had to wait two weeks before I could grit my teeth and shout as I put my weight on my incapacitated side and eased myself into the saddle. It felt great and I was only going to walk around the road on Charlie as I haven't come off him yet. That is all I did, but at least I found out that I still wanted to ride. I was still quite incapacitated, so someone from home would take me up to Stibb Cross, where I got the school bus into the school where I work. The children on the 'boogie bus' (so called because the radio was blaring out pop songs on the journeys to and from school) were brilliant and ran around opening doors and helping me. I also had to use a walking stick for a month. I used to limp around the office because I thought the more I moved around, the better it would get, and I was right! When the pain had finally eased enough so that I could go to my chiropractor to see what injuries I had actually sustained, he told me that I had pulled my left leg out of its socket to the point of dislocation! He told me to be careful about riding, and had a fit when I told him that I was already back in the saddle, but then he thought about it and he said he wasn't surprised, knowing me! That was the last time I was going to try and sort out youngsters, especially big 17.2hh youngsters. We finally took Toby up to a local eventing yard, where they schooled him on and he was eventually bought by a nice couple down in Cornwall for hunting and eventing, and the last I heard was doing very well.

Tinern's next foal was Tintern Tufty, so named because he had a tuft of hair on his chin – very ingenious). Again, Ron broke him in and Beccy rode him on for a bit (since by this time, we had lost Splodge). We hacked him and took him indoor-jumping locally, where he went very well. As we did not want to sell him, we decided to loan him out to go eventing, but never again would I consider doing such a thing. The person that wanted him on loan could 'talk the talk' and so we thought she could 'walk the walk', but no way could she 'ride the ride'. They were going to keep him at an eventing yard near Newton Abbot and the owner was a respected eventer, so we were happy as the girl and her mother told us that she was having lessons there. When she came up to 'try him out', she didn't look too bad. She took him up and down the road looking the part and was quite strong and confident. The only thing was that when she went to jump him in the sand paddock, he ducked out the last minute and she went sailing into the mud and water. It was quite a funny sight but I suppose the writing was on the wall then, but obviously in invisible ink as far as I was concerned! Mother said, "Oh, she won't care," and indeed she got back on and took Tufty around the sand paddock and over some jumps. The owner of the yard herself came up and collected Tufty and it looked quite promising until we went down to the stable a week later to see how everything was progressing.

We arrived around midday and found the actual yard to be very nice, but it soon became obvious that the 'loanee' wasn't anything to do with it and in fact, only rented a stable there – a draughty one, come to that. The rented stables were well away from the rest of the yard and we were not that happy when we came away. I did not hear anything for another week, but they rang me on the Saturday to say that Tufty had thrown her off. He had never done anything like that in his life before. Apparently the girl (and I use the term girl quite loosely as she was well into her twenties and quite large) was black and blue and obviously could not ride. Tufty knew it as well, and consequently, she lost her nerve completely and didn't want to ride him again. So they brought him home.

We then decided to send Tufty to the eventing yard in Hatherleigh to be schooled on. In fact they asked us if we had considered keeping him and eventing him as he could go on to be fairly useful. We were not in a position to do that then, and as they knew of someone who wanted a horse for their daughter, we were asked if we would consider loaning him again. Despite the previous experience, we agreed, and the new people, again from the Newton Abbot area, drew up a contract. They took him away, but it seemed that yet again, they were people who had no idea about horse management and were soon telling us that Tufty was so petrified of travelling that they had to turn round and go home when trying to take him to a show. This all seemed very strange to us as we had been taking him to shows for the previous year without any problems, so back he came again. That is seriously the last time that I would ever loan a horse. Tufty was finally bought by some lovely people who owned a hotel, near Camelford. They loved him to pieces and when they went away on holiday they sent him up to Hatherleigh so that he could be exercised.

The next foal turned out to be twins! Ron had fitted up a video in the stable and though he kept looking every two hours through the night, he still missed the birth. When he went down to the stable Tintern had had twins. The bigger one was okay, but the second foal was about the size of a dog, but sadly, it died. One was chestnut and the other one was a lovely bay (or so Ron said). I, of course did not want to see the foal that had not survived, but Ron said it was perfectly formed. It was probably just as well that it did not survive, as they always turn out to be sickly and have a lot of things go wrong with them. I thought we were lucky to have a living foal out of twins as they are usually aborted at seven months as a rule. So now we had Tintern Twinkle. Being one of twins she did not grow as big as her siblings but she made around 16 hands. Ron broke her in and one of our farmer friends came up, backed her and rode out with us on several occasions. He liked her so much that he bought her and so she lives locally (about 4 miles away) and we still see her. She is a very good all-rounder. Our farmer friend, Daniel, initially had her for hunting, but he has show jumped her and his wife rides her as well. Like all of Tintern's foals, sired by Tobias Corbett, she absolutely adores jumping.

Then we decided (I know not why) to use a Thoroughbred stallion on the mare, and so we went to look around the stud and picked Kuwait Beach, a beautiful grey (I suspect that had a lot to do with the selection of the stallion, as I love the grey colour, but Ron did agree with me thank goodness). I thought that maybe we stood a chance of breeding either an eventer or a racehorse.

This is what it says about Kuwait Beach on futuresporthorses.co.uk: "Kuwait Beach is the renowned sire of top-drawer event horses including Ingrid Klimke's Olympic horse Sleep Late. Kuwait Beach was ranked 3rd by the World Breeding Federation as an event sire and consistently produces athletic, trainable horses that go on to excel in all disciplines. This comes as no surprise when you look at Kuwait himself. Neat, correct conformation is coupled with beautiful limbs and the elevated, athletic paces we are more used to seeing in modern day warm-bloods.

As a racehorse, he proved very tough and consistent running 13 times and, under the old H.I.S. scheme, was a winner at Newmarket of both Premiums and Super Premiums. His successful eventing progeny are in abundance, the most famous Sleep Late won individual silver in the 2000 Sydney Olympics for Germany in the 3-day event. Ritzy Pitzy, Sarnllys Helena, Mid Day Sun, High Robins and Star Turn II are all Advanced. Consistent dressage winners include Chiltern Beech (157 pts) and Denchworth Chieftan (120 pts), while in the show ring Kuwait's children are equally impressive. Gulf Crisis is one of the most prolific winning small hunters of recent years, while Khubla Khan flies the flag in the lightweights, and Mystiko, Beach Bay and Penarth Blue Steel ensure that Kuwait is well represented in the heavyweight divisions. All are county winners in their own right and regular visitors to the Horse Of The Year Show at Wembley."

We were so pleased when Tintern had the most beautiful foal, a dark bay filly with a lovely white blaze. All went well for the first day but as time went on, sadly it became apparent that there was something drastically wrong with the foal. She was having difficulty standing up and when she did she was – and I can only describe it as – paddling on the spot. After a day we called the vet who could not find anything wrong with her. Ron was getting her up and holding her so that she could suckle the mare's milk, but things did not improve. The next day at about 10pm, Ron went down to get her up to suckle but she was not good. He shouted to me to get the vet and of course these days you cannot call straight through, you have to go through an emergency call centre and then wait for the vet to call you back. As I ran back to call Ron shouted, "Tell them that if they are not here in the next half an hour she will be dead!" Luckily, the vet on call was a good one who knew where we lived, and proceeded post haste and arrived within half an hour. Of course, there was nothing he could do and he was still at a loss to know what was wrong. He asked if we would be prepared to bring her in for a post mortem. Ron took her in and the vet rang the next day to say that they still could not find the cause and could only presume that there was some sort of abnormality in her brain. I was devastated and it will never be known whether we would have bred a show horse, racehorse, or eventer.

The next time that Tintern went back to stud we went back to our old favourite, Tobias Corbett and we now have the last of her progeny, Tintern Tinker. He was expected to grow to approximately 17.2hh, but now stands at 18.3hh and is 8-years-old.

Alas, poor Tintern had always had a big knee and she unfortunately tripped in the field one day and injured it again. We decided that she had done enough breeding and retired her until we deemed her knee that bad that we were afraid that if she tripped we would come down and find her with a broken leg. We asked the advice of our vet who told us that unfortunately, there was nothing he could do for her We said goodbye to Tintern and like all the animals we have lost at home, she is buried on our land.

# TINTERN TINKER

Tinker certainly never gave any impression that he was going to grow into the great big animal that he is. The biggest horse I had seen before him was at the event yard near Hatherleigh. He belonged to an American and was a big grey Thoroughbred over 18hh nicknamed 'Alp' for obvious reasons!

Tinker was treated the same as any other one of our foals, and eventually it was possible to groom him in the middle of the field and pick his feet up etc. It took quite a lot of work to get him like that but, when you know that the horses are going to be big, you have to start their education when they are small! Ron began to break Tinker in when he was 2-years-old, very gently because with big horses they are physically generally a year behind the smaller horses, and their bones take longer to fuse together. We brought him on slowly and Ron long-reined him and then we sent up to the event yard to be backed and 'ridden-on'. We talked about it and then decided that, as he was our last foal and we had lost Tintern Memory and the stallion was deceased, we should like to see if he would make an eventer.

His first event was at Moreton in Dorset. We were going to travel down on the Saturday but I thought it would be better to go and stay the night so that we were close at hand instead of rushing about, so we stayed at Lulworth Cove. What a lovely place. Tinks' dressage was in the afternoon, and so we got to the event at ten in the morning. Sophie, who had been schooling him was going to ride him. She lunged him for quite a while in the morning as it was his first time and no one knew how he was going to react. Well, he was as good as gold. Just before he entered the dressage arena, it poured heavily with rain, but poor old Sophie was doggedly schooling Tinker in all of this. He was first to go after lunch and we watched with bated breath. Considering he did not know what to expect, he did a wonderful job. In fact, that was probably why! He had a score of 29.5, which everyone was overjoyed about and he has never been in the 20s since! Next came the show jumping. He had 12 jumping faults and 7 time faults. We were very pleased as it was a small, enclosed, arena and he was a big baby of just 5-years-old.

Next was his *pièce de résistance*, the cross-country! All of Tobias Corbett's offspring had been good at cross-country, though it is a different thing in an actual event rather than practicing at home. Sophie was only going to take him gently (she thought), as it was his first time. My heart was in my mouth when he set off as there were some really big jumps and especially the last where he had to jump through a huge horseshoe. He went round clear, and came home very tired as he had had a long day. Sophie was standing up in the saddle throwing her arms aloft and I went running to her in tears as she pulled him up. We were so pleased that the only thing that had ended in tears was me, and nothing else as the saying goes! He was scheduled to go to Longleat in the next fortnight, but as I was to find out over the next three years, nothing ever goes according to plan with horses, and he unfortunately got a foot injury, which manifested itself as a big hole in his hoof and so therefore, was sidelined for the next few weeks.

One month later he went to Winkleigh and competed in the next class up, but he now knew the form and was a naughty boy. His dressage score was 47, he had 4 down in the show jumping, was clear cross-country but had 31.2 time faults.

Two weeks later he went to Stockland Lovell and finished 8th – a rosette! He had 42 dressage points (never to be his strong point – he is so big and the arena so small) but was clear in the other two elements. Next was Nutwell Court. What an absolutely awful day – the usual English summer – hammering down with rain, but despite the weather, Tinks went well: 39 dressage points (below 40 so I was pleased) only one down show jumping and 5.2 time faults cross-country. Sophie came back soaked to the skin, but over the moon and declared that he was a 'cross-country machine'. The gremlins stepped in for the rest of the year's events: we were away on the beautiful island of Crete when Tinks was next competing at the event held in his yard, but at least we didn't have the usual travelling expenses – hoorah! We always stay with a friend in Oxfordshire on August Bank Holiday weekend so we couldn't be with him to see him compete on that day either. However, my friend Sylvie had arranged for me to go to her friend's house, who had a computer so that I could look up the result. Ron was really confident that he would do well, especially as he had the advantage of home ground! Well, I looked on the computer and my heart skipped a beat: HF (horse fall). I dashed back to Ron and Sylv, my imagination running wild (and believe me, I have got one), fearing the worst: that he had turned 'topsy turvy' over a jump and squashed Sophie or some other such horrible thing. I rang the yard as soon as I got back and I was told that he had fallen on the flat, trotting through water and had crossed his legs in a tractor rut and just gone down. Nothing worse than an ear-full of water and another soaking for poor Sophie, who was devastated, but both horse and rider were fine. Phew! He was then entered for Dauntsy Park but caught a bad cold and so there endeth the 2009 Eventing Season for Tinks, but out of four starts he had a rosette. What a brilliant result.

At the start of 2010 we were told that there was a new rider in the yard, a French man by the name of Xavier. We were not too happy, as we wanted Sophie to continue to ride him, but it shows how much we know, as we were totally new to eventing. Tinker was obviously bigger and stronger, and at 18.1hh was quite a handful for a small girl to ride, so they thought it for the best and of course it was. Sophie had given him a lovely gentle start and had done well with him and now it was time to move on. Funnily enough, though, on Xavier and Tinker's first outing at Bickenhall, Xavier came off a previous ride and broke his collarbone and so Sophie rode Tinker after all. He was very naughty 54 D, 16 SJ and clear but 26 time faults XC, but even then he finished 25th. It seemed he really did need a stronger person to ride him, and anyway, Sophie left the yard and went to work in another riding environment to earn more money to enable her to afford her own eventer.

Xavier got Tinks going really well and won several rosettes with him in 2011. In July he went to his second novice event at Barbury. What a beautiful place. It poured with rain for the dressage and it was not such a good test. He did the best show jumping round that I had ever seen and then went clear on a stiff cross-country course built by Captain Mark Philips. Xavier came back 'over the moon' as Tinks had just earned his 1st BE point with a double clear. Things were going well, but it was a case of first the ups and then the downs! Tinks fell and squashed Xavier while schooling the ménage. It was decided that he didn't look "quite right" and so the vet was called and the said that he did not know how Tinker had competed at Barbury as he only had one sound leg, thus proving what an honest horse he is. That, then, was the end of the 2011 season for us and Tinker, as he was diagnosed with a suspensory ligament injury and his coffin bones did not look correct on X-ray. He needed complete rest, and painkillers, and special bar shoes on the front and built up shoes behind. These cost a fortune and had to be specially made for such a big horse.

We came back from a holiday to the bad news (for us) that Xavier had been headhunted by a top French rider and had left the yard and gone back to France. We met the new 'jockey', Yann, who is a delightful person, but firstly he had to build up a relationship with Tinker all over again (and that does not happen in five minutes). 2012 was the most awful year for eventing with most of Tinker's events cancelled because of the wet weather. It is very difficult to keep a horse at its peak of fitness to compete and then the event is cancelled. Two weeks later the same thing happened again, even Badminton was cancelled. When Tinker did finally manage to compete and was lying in 4th place with XC to go (which was a 'banker' for us as XC is his forte), the old adage "never count your chickens" springs to mind. He threw a back shoe while on awful, muddy, slippery, sliding ground, and half way round the course, crashed onto his side and onto poor Yann. Tinker was shaken and fairly 'stirred', and so was Yann; he was looking a bit spaced-out when he was brought back to the medics. He had four more horses to ride in the novice classes and said that he was okay to carry on but was holding an icepack to his knee. He managed the dressage but then had to withdraw and subsequently, could not ride for three weeks. I don't think his knee will never be the same again. He did compete Tinker again, and we were pleased with the result after that awful fall, as Tinker did not seem to be 'fazed' about the XC at all.

He was taken to one last event up in Warwickshire, so they set off at 3.00am and he was competing at 8.30am. He did not do well in the jumping and went down on to his knees again on the awful ground, ending up with sore shins, and that was the end of an awful season for all concerned.

So now, although he is still at the yard, he is having a rest until the start of the next season and whatever lies beyond! Fingers and hooves crossed!

# MY JOURNEY

Now I've completed my Memoir, I realise that I've been on two wonderful interwoven journeys: one to connect with my heritage and family in Estonia – what joy that has brought Ron and I; and the other to recall all the wonderful and challenging relationships I've had with my horses over the years, and the fascinating people I have met along the way. Estonia and Equines have been my life – I hope you enjoyed the ride.

Tintern Tinker 2013

Printed in Great Britain
by Amazon.co.uk, Ltd.,
Marston Gate.